T0225132

Quick Functional Programming

Why learn functional programming? Isn't that some complicated ivory-tower technique used only in obscure languages like Haskell?

In fact, functional programming is actually very simple. It's also very powerful, as Haskell demonstrates by throwing away all the conventional programming tools and using only functional programming features. But it doesn't have to be done that way.

Functional programming is a power tool that you can use in addition to all your usual tools, to whatever extent your current mainstream language supports it. Most languages have at least basic support.

In this book, we use Python and Java and, as a bonus, Scala. If you prefer another language, there will be minor differences in syntax, but the concepts are the same.

Give functional programming a try. You may be surprised how much a single power tool can help you in your day-to-day programming.

Quick Functional Programming

David Matuszek

CRC Press
Taylor & Francis Group
Boca Raton London New York

CRC Press is an imprint of the
Taylor & Francis Group, an **informa** business
A CHAPMAN & HALL BOOK

First edition published 2023
by CRC Press
6000 Broken Sound Parkway NW, Suite 300, Boca Raton, FL 33487-2742

and by CRC Press
4 Park Square, Milton Park, Abingdon, Oxon, OX14 4RN

CRC Press is an imprint of Taylor & Francis Group, LLC

© 2023 David Matuszek

ISBN: 978-1-032-41532-1 (hbk)
ISBN: 978-1-032-41531-4 (pbk)
ISBN: 978-1-003-35854-1 (ebk)

DOI: 10.1201/9781003358541

Typeset in Minion
by SPi Technologies India Pvt Ltd (Straive)

To all my students,
past, present, and future.

Contents

About the Author

I'M **DAVID MATUSZEK**, known to most of my students as "Dr. Dave."

I wrote my first program on punched cards in 1963 and immediately got hooked.

I taught my first computer classes in 1970, as a graduate student in Computer Science at The University of Texas in Austin. I eventually got my PhD from there, and I've been teaching ever since. Admittedly, I spent over a dozen years in industry, but even then, I taught as an adjunct for Villanova university.

I finally escaped from industry and joined the Villanova faculty full time for a few years and then moved to the University of Pennsylvania, where I directed a Master's program (MCIT, Masters in Computer and Information Technology) for students coming into computer science from another discipline.

Throughout my career, my main interests have been in artificial intelligence (AI) and programming languages. I've used a lot of programming languages.

I retired in 2017, but I can't stop teaching, so I'm writing a series of "quick start" books on programming and programming languages. I've also written two science fiction novels, *Ice Jockey* and *All True Value*, and I expect to write more. Check them out!

And hey, if you're a former student of mine, drop me a note. I'd love to hear from you!

david.matuszek@gmail.com

Preface

YOU PROBABLY THINK THAT *functional programming* (*FP*) is something dreamed up by ivory-tower academics using obscure languages that few people understand.

You're right.

You probably think that those weird languages such as Haskell, Standard ML, and OCaml are never going to be very popular with ordinary programmers.

Right again.

But did you notice...

- That ivory-tower academics are some pretty smart people?
- That the programming language you use every day, whatever it is, is getting more FP features?

"Pure" functional programming, abandoning all the conventional programming techniques, really is difficult. But you don't have to do that. Think of it this way: Conventional programming consists of a collection of hand tools, and FP adds a power tool to the mix. Just one—it doesn't do everything, and you still need all the other tools (unless you're an ivory-tower academic), but where you can use it, it saves a lot of work.

Here's a spoiler: FP will let you replace many of your loops with shorter, simpler, easier to understand function calls. Yes, there's some unfamiliar syntax involved, but it's just syntax, and you can get used to it very quickly. The new concepts, the parts you might think are the most difficult, turn out to be trivially simple.

You may be surprised how much a single power tool can help you in your day-to-day programming.

FP is coming into prominence now because it is a far better way to write concurrent programs, suitable for multi-core computers. However, this is only a book about functional programming, *not* about concurrent programming; that would require a far larger volume.

Each chapter after the first begins with an explanation of some particular concept of functional programming. After that, there are sections exemplifying that concept in each of three languages.

- **Python**, because it is a simple, widely known language. Python has only a few of the most basic FP features.

- **Java**, because it is widely known and has many of the FP features. The developers of these features have done an awesome job in fitting these features into a language that was never designed to hold them.

- **Scala**, which has been designed from the ground up to be both object oriented and functional, and therefore provides the cleanest and most complete set of FP features.

I have tried to make this book accessible to programmers who do not know Python or Scala. The FP features of these languages can be understood without an in-depth knowledge of the language in which they occur. Unfortunately, no such claim can be made for Java.

## CHAPTER 1

What Is Functional Programming?

A MATHEMATICAL FUNCTION HAS ARGUMENTS, and from those arguments, it computes a result. Given the same arguments again, it will produce the same result, every time. Consequently,

- A function uses its arguments, and only its arguments, to produce a result. It has no access to "global variables," random numbers, the time of day, or anything like that.

- A function has no *side effects*. It does not change anything in its environment. It does not change the values of its arguments. It does no input or output.

- A function has *referential transparency*. Once the value of a function with certain arguments has been computed, then any call to the function with those arguments, in any context, may be replaced by that value.

A function with the above characteristics is called a *pure function*.

DOI: 10.1201/9781003358541-1

In a functional language, *functions are values.* This means that they can be stored in variables, passed around as parameters, and returned as the result of a function calls, just like any other type of value. There are even operations on functions that produce new functions.

Almost any programming language has functions, of course, but in functional programming, the entire program is thought of as being a function that has functions within it.

Obviously, programs need the ability to do input and output. One reason purely functional languages such as Haskell are difficult is that they require input/output to be put in a "walled garden" where they don't have to be seen by the rest of the code. The ability of Haskell to do this is something of an intellectual feat, but its practical value is controversial.

Another important idea from mathematics is that *variables don't vary.* If the value of a variable x is known, it has the same value throughout the computation. If you want to model a process that changes over time, you might say $x' = f(x)$, where x' is a "new" value; but it is also in a new variable, x'.

To model this in programming terms, we say that variables have to be **single assignment**—once given a value, that value cannot be changed. In addition, that value must be **immutable**; for example, it cannot be an array whose elements can be changed.

The single-assignment property means that we need some way to create new variables; not only x but also x', x'', x''', and so on for as many variables as we need. This is easily done with recursion, because every recursive call creates a new set of variables. Loops, on the other hand, are used almost exclusively to *change* values, which is contrary to the functional programming view. Because any task that can be accomplished with loops can also be done with recursion, functional programming uses recursion rather than loops.

Because values must be immutable, memory demands for new values can be high. This is dealt with by automatically **garbage collecting** values that are no longer needed and by using **persistent** data structures: A change to one part of the data structure does not require making a complete copy of the parts that have not changed.

Another consequence is that functional programming is **expression-oriented** rather than **statement-oriented**. An entire program may consist of a single expression, along with definitions of variables and functions (which themselves consist of single expressions).

In summary, pure functional programming requires that:

- Functions are pure and can be treated as values.

- Variables are single-assignment, and values are immutable.

- Recursion is used in preference to loops.

- Garbage collection is automatic and data structures are persistent.

- Programs are expression-oriented rather than statement-oriented.

Pure functional programming can be done in specialized languages such as Haskell and OCaml. For the practicing programmer, however, such purity is unattainable in conventional languages. This is not without its advantages; all the usual programming tools, including loops, can be employed, while also making use of functional programming features when they are appropriate.

The reader may question why a less common language such as Scala is included in this book. Python supports only the most basic functional features; Java supports more features, but at the cost of considerable added complexity; and purely functional languages such as Haskell seem downright "weird" to most programmers. Scala has an almost complete set of functional programming features, but the syntax is much closer to that of mainstream languages, so the Scala examples should be fairly easy to understand.

CHAPTER **2**

Methods and Functions

A **METHOD** BELONGS TO AN object. It has access to the fields of the object and can read and modify them. It can use other methods in that object.

A *function* is, or should be, independent of the context in which it occurs. It should use only its arguments in computing a result; it should have no side effects; and it should have referential transparency.

Of course, not all methods access the fields or call other methods of the object that owns them, and not all functions are "pure" in the above sense.

One of the chief advantages of pure functions is that their correctness can be verified without taking context into account. This makes pure functions much easier to debug. Another advantage is that, since pure functions do not depend on context, they can be passed around as freely as any other kind of value.

DOI: 10.1201/9781003358541-2

2.1 METHODS

The following sections summarize the syntax used for declaring and using methods and describe how methods can sometimes be used in place of functions.

2.1.1 Methods in Python

Here is how you would define a simple method in Python:

```python
def plus(a, b):
    return a + b
```

A call to this method might look like this: `c = plus(a, b)`.

In Python, the types of variables are not declared. The `plus` method can be applied to integers, reals, or strings, since all of these have a + operator.

We can show that the `plus` method is a value by copying it into another variable:

```python
sum = plus
```

Following this assignment, the statement `c = sum(a, b)` does exactly the same thing as `c = plus(a, b)`.

Python is object oriented, so it has methods, and Python lets us use them much like functions. Methods are defined within a class, while functions are defined external to any class.

Here is a class definition:

```python
class Arithmetic():

    # Instance method
    def plus1(self, a, b):
        return a + b
```

```
@staticmethod
def plus2(a, b):
    return a + b
```

In the above class definition, plus1 is an instance method, so that it belongs to every object created from the Arithmetic class. The particular object can be referenced inside the method via the variable self, though that is not done in this example. To use this method, prefix it with the name of the object that owns it, followed by a dot.

```
obj = Arithmetic() # Creates an object
print(obj.plus1(1, 2)) # Prints 3
```

Even though obj.plus1 is a method, not a function, we can assign it to a new variable.

```
sum1 = obj.plus1
print(sum1(3, 4)) # Prints 7
```

A "static" method is essentially a function. Since another class could define a method with the same name, you have to say in which class plus2 is defined; however, it has no special access to the fields or methods of that class.

```
print(Arithmetic.plus2(5, 6)) # Prints 11
```

Similarly, just as we can assign obj.plus1 to a new variable, we can assign Arithmetic.plus2 to a new variable.

```
sum2 = Arithmetic.plus2
print(sum2(7, 8)) # Prints 15
```

2.1.2 Methods in Java

A typical Java method looks like this:

```
public static int plus(int a, int b) {
  return a + b;
}
```

Here, the initial int specifies the type of value returned from the method; static means that it can be used directly from the class, without first creating an object; plus is the name of the method; and the parameters are both of type int. The next line calculates a return value, which also must be of type int.

If this were a function, you could call it directly. Instead, you have to define a class containing the method and then tell the class (formally, *send a message to the class*) to execute the method. Or you could create an object of that class and then send the message plus to the object. Either way, the method doesn't exist as an independent function.

Java has the operator : : for converting a method to a function. If the above method is defined in class FP, the corresponding function is FP::plus. It can be used as follows:

```
IntBinaryOperator sum = FP::plus;
System.out.println(sum.applyAsInt(3, 4));
```

The above code will print 7.

Briefly, functions that take two ints as parameters and produce an int result must implement the IntBinaryOperator interface. The method defined by this interface is applyAsInt. This type of interface is one of many that will be explained in detail later.

Because sum is a function and functions are values, we can assign it to another variable of the same type:

```
IntBinaryOperator sum2 = sum;
System.out.println(sum2.applyAsInt(3, 4));
```

Since sum2 is the same as sum, this code will also print 7.

2.1.3 Methods in Scala

Scala has both methods and functions.

Here is how you would define a simple method in Scala:

```
def plus(a: Int, b: Int) = a + b
```

The method is named plus, and the two parameters a and b are both declared to be of type Int (integer). The result of the computation is the sum of a and b, and Scala can deduce that it has type Int.

Note: All values in Scala are objects; there are no "primitives."

The method body follows the equals sign. If the method body consists of more than a single expression, it is enclosed in braces, {}. The value returned by the method is the value of the last expression in the method body.

Methods can often be used where a function is expected.

```
def apply(fun: (Int, Int) => Int, a: Int, b: Int) =
    fun(a, b)

apply(plus, 3, 4) // Prints 7
```

The apply method expects a function fun as a parameter. The notation (Int, Int) => Int indicates the *type* of fun is a function that takes two integer parameters and returns an integer result.

Methods are not values and cannot always be used in place of functions. In particular, a method cannot be assigned to a new variable. The workaround is to convert the method to a function by following it with a single underscore.

Examples:

```
val add = plus _    // note underscore
println(plus(1, 2)) // prints 3
println(add(3, 4))  // prints 7
```

In functional programming, variables don't vary. Once a value has been assigned to a variable, that value in that variable cannot be changed—it is **immutable.**

Because Scala has strong support for functional programming, but doesn't insist on it, there are two ways to declare variables. A variable declared with val (value) is immutable, while a variable declared with var (variable) is the usual kind of **mutable** variable—it can be reassigned at will. It is good technique to declare variables with val and only change the declaration to var if it becomes necessary. In a completely functional program, this would never become necessary.

When declaring a variable, there is no need to specify its type (though you may). Scala determines this from the value assigned to the variable.

2.2 FUNCTION LITERALS

A **function literal** is kind of a "lightweight" function. It is a way of writing a function without necessarily giving it a name, so it is sometimes called an **anonymous function.**

Function literals are values. They can be assigned to variables, but a function literal is often used only in one place and just written where it is needed. Function literals are most often used as arguments in a function call.

The body of a function literal can be any length, but is most often just a single expression. When the function is called, the expression is evaluated and the result returned as the value of the function.

Function literals do not add any "power" to a language. Instead, their purpose is to provide a notation that is more concise, easier to write, and easier to read.

Scala is expression oriented; in theory, a single expression can be arbitrarily complex. However, as a matter of style, function literals should be kept short, typically not more than a single line.

2.2.1 Function Literals in Python

In Python, a function literal to add two numbers looks like this:

```
lambda a, b: a + b
```

Instead of beginning with the keyword def and a name, a function literal begins with the keyword lambda. Then, there are zero or more parameters, an equals sign, and an expression. The value of the expression will be the result returned by the function. (The keyword lambda was chosen for historical reasons.)

A literal function has no name and no scope, just as the integer literal 5 has no name and no scope. It is a value that can be used in an expression or as an expression all by itself.

Although a function literal starts out as an anonymous function, it can be saved in a variable and used that way.

```
plus = lambda a, b: a + b
print(plus(3, 4)) # prints 7
```

But since a function literal *is* a function, it can be used without first giving it a name.

```
print((lambda a, b: a + b)(3, 4)) # prints 7
```

The most common use of a function literal is as an argument to another function.

```
def combine(fun, a):
    result = a[0]
    for i in range(1, len(a)):
        result = fun(result, a[i])
    return result

a = [1, 20, 300]
print(combine(lambda a, b: a + b, a)) # prints 321
print(combine(lambda a, b: a * b, a)) # prints 6000
```

2.2.2 Function Literals in Java

Starting in Java 8, you can define a function literal as follows:

(*parameters*) -> *expression_or_block*

It is sometimes required to specify parameter types, as in a method definition (int a, etc.). In many cases, the types may be omitted, and Java can determine them.

If there is only one parameter, and its type is not specified, the parentheses may be omitted. If there are no parameters, empty parentheses are required.

The body of the function can be either a single expression or a block of statements enclosed in braces, {}. In the latter case, it must contain one or more return statements to specify the value of the function.

A function literal to add two numbers looks like this:

```
(a, b) -> a + b
```

In order to use this literal function, it must be given a name, and that name must have the correct type. If the intent is to add integers and get an integer result, the type name is IntBinaryOperator.

But it's more complicated than this. IntBinaryOperator is the name of an interface, and that interface defines an abstract method applyAsInt. To make this work, we save the function in a variable of type IntBinaryOperator and then "send a message to" (i.e., call) the abstract method.

```
IntBinaryOperator add = (x, y) -> x + y;
System.out.println(add.applyAsInt(3, 4)); // prints 7
```

The requirement to have a name for every possible function type adds considerably to the complexity of using function literals in Java. Section 4.6, *Provided Functional Interfaces*, lists and describes 43 types, but you can also define your own.

2.2.3 Function Literals in Scala

Function literals in Scala are defined using the syntax (*parameters*) => *expression*. Every parameter must have a specified type.

```
val subtract = (a: Int, b: Int) => a - b
```

The return type is not required, but may be provided.

```
val subtract = (a: Int, b: Int): Int => a - b
```

The type of a function is easily specified: Just leave out the variable names. For example, the type of subtract is (Int, Int) => Int.

Scala requires that method and function parameters must specify their type. For example, if you want to pass subtract as a parameter to method doIt, the method definition would look like this:

```
def doIt(fn: (Int, Int) => Int,
         x: Int, y: Int) = fn(x, y)
```

The call doIt(subtract, 10, 3) will return 7.

More complex Scala function literals may be enclosed in braces; the return value is the last value computed.

2.3 SORTING EXAMPLES

The examples provided thus far have been trivial. It's time for some more compelling examples.

Most programming languages will provide a library method for sorting an array into ascending order. Occasionally, however, some other form of sorting is needed, and the provided method is useless. The programmer must then write a completely new sorting method, even though the only change needed is to determine which of two values should precede the other. This determination can easily be made by a function that is supplied as a parameter.

2.3.1 Sorting in Python

The following code is based on a standard *insertion sort*. There is no need to understand in detail how it works; the important points to notice are the inclusion of a parameter named precedes and the replacement of the test n < a[j - 1] with the function call precedes (n, a[j - 1]).

```
def fun_sort(a, precedes):
    i = 1
    while i < len(a):
        n = a[i]
        j = i
        i = i + 1
        while j > 0 and precedes(n, a[j - 1]):
            a[j] = a[j - 1]
            j = j - 1
        a[j] = n
```

We can use this to sort list numbers from smallest to largest by supplying smaller as a parameter.

```
def smaller(a, b):
    return a < b

fun_sort(numbers, smaller)
```

By using function literals, even the need to provide a separate smaller function is eliminated.

```
fun_sort(numbers, lambda a, b: a < b)
```

We can use fun_sort to sort an array in descending order:

```
fun_sort(numbers, lambda a, b: a > b)
```

We can sort all odd numbers before all even numbers:

```
fun_sort(numbers,
    lambda a, b: a % 2 > b % 2
```

We can sort according to the last (ones) digit:

```
fun_sort(numbers, lambda a, b: a % 10 < b % 10)
```

We can sort according to the number of factors a number has:

```
fun_sort(numbers,
    lambda a, b: n_factors(a) < n_factors(b))
```

Additional uses can easily be imagined. Since Python is a dynamically typed language, fun_sort can be applied to almost any list of values.

2.3.2 Sorting in Java

Numbers and strings have a predefined *natural ordering*. To sort an array of numbers or of strings, we can use the sort method in java.util.Arrays. This sorts the array in place; it does not return a new array.

To define a "natural ordering" for any objects we create, the class defining the objects should implement the Comparable interface and provide a compareTo(*object*) method.

But Comparable is limited because each type of object can have only one natural ordering. For more flexibility, the java.util.Arrays class also provides a sort method with the following signature:

```
sort(T[] a, Comparator<? super T> c)
```

This means, roughly speaking, that it will sort an array a of values of type T, or any subclass of type T, according to a "Comparator" c.

Assume that we have a Planet class, where each Planet has a name, an integer location that tells where it is in order from the sun (Earth is third), and a floating-point mass.

If we want to sort planets in various ways, the traditional way of doing this is to provide a Comparator class for each way we might want to sort the Planets. To sort by location, here is a possible Comparator.

```
public class PlanetLocationComparator<T>
    implements java.util.Comparator<T> {

    @Override
    public int compare(T o1, T o2) {
        Planet p1 = (Planet)o1;
        Planet p2 = (Planet)o2;
        return p1.location - p2.location;
    }
}
```

We can use this Comparator to sort an array of planets.

```
PlanetLocationComparator<Planet> locationSorter =
    new PlanetLocationComparator<Planet>();
Arrays.sort(planets, locationSorter);
```

To sort planets by name, we would have to define another Comparator class. If we wanted to sort in other ways, for example by mass or by diameter, we would need still more Comparator classes.

A Comparator is a *functional interface*; these will be described in detail in Section 4. For now, it is enough to say that we can supply a function literal as the second parameter to sort. This means that we can replace all of the above code with the following:

```
Arrays.sort(planets,
    (p1, p2) -> p1.location - p2.location);
```

A Comparator has to return an integer value. The result should be negative if the first argument is smaller, zero if they are equal, and positive if the first argument is greater. Our location comparator did exactly this.

Comparisons by mass, which is a double value, are somewhat more complicated. If we simply cast each mass to an integer before comparison, different masses could result in the same integer. The solution is to do the subtraction using doubles, but use the signum function to convert this difference to −1.0, 0.0, or +1.0 and then cast the result to an integer.

```
Arrays.sort(planets, (p1, p2) ->
    (int)java.lang.Math.signum(p1.mass - p2.mass));
```

Strings have a natural ordering, so they have a compareTo method. Fortunately, compareTo is also a functional interface.

```
Arrays.sort(planets, (p1, p2) ->
    p1.name.compareTo(p2.name));
```

2.3.3 Sorting in Scala

Scala provides a sorted method which will sort a sequence according to its **natural order**. The natural order for numbers and strings is what you would probably expect; it can be defined for other types of objects.

Of more interest to us, Scala also provides a sortWith method. Methods belong to objects and are called with **dot syntax**; so, to sort an object such as a list, we would say:

object.sortWith(**function**)

If we have a list of integers, we can sort it however we like. All we need to do is provide it with a function of two parameters, which will return true if the value given to the first parameter should precede the value given to the second parameter.

```
val numbers = List(31, 41, 59, 26, 53, 49, 16)
println(numbers.sortWith((a: Int, b: Int) => a < b))
// prints List(16, 26, 31, 41, 49, 53, 59)

println(numbers.sortWith((a: Int, b: Int) => a > b))
// prints List(59, 53, 49, 41, 31, 26, 16)

println(numbers.sortWith((a: Int, b: Int) =>
                a % 10 < b % 10))
// prints List(31, 41, 53, 26, 16, 59, 49)
```

The last of these sorts the numbers according to their last digit.

The above examples used a list of integers. We can sort objects of any type, for example, strings.

```
val languages = List("Python", "Java", "Scala")
println(languages.sortWith(
        (a: String, b: String) => a < b))
// prints List(Java, Python, Scala)

println(languages.sortWith(
        (a: String, b: String) => a.length < b.length))
// prints List(Java, Scala, Python)
```

As Scala is designed to be functional, sortWith always returns a new list; it doesn't modify the given list.

## CHAPTER 3

Higher-Order Functions

A FUNCTION THAT TAKES ANOTHER function as a parameter, or returns a function as a result, is known as a **higher-order function**. This name somehow makes the function seem special. It isn't. We don't have a special name for a function that takes an integer as an argument or returns an integer as a value, so why have a special name for a function that takes or returns functions?

The purpose of giving a parameter to a function is to specialize that function; that is, apply it to specific data. This remains true when the parameter is itself a function.

In Section 2.3, we saw how a single sorting algorithm could be specialized to sort an array or list according to almost any criteria, simply by giving the method an appropriate function to compare two values.

Often it is necessary to reduce an array or list to a single value: the largest or smallest value, the sum or product of all the values, or

DOI: 10.1201/9781003358541-3

perhaps the number of elements in the array or list. In the following sections, we will write a single function that can do all of these things, simply by giving it a function that combines two values into one.

3.1 HIGHER-ORDER FUNCTIONS IN PYTHON

To add up the elements of a list, or to find the least and greatest element, Python already has the functions sum, min, and max. (A Python list is like an array in other languages.) It doesn't come with a product method to multiply together all the elements of a list, but we could write one like this:

```python
def product(lst):
    result = lst[0]
    for i in range(1, len(lst)):
        result = result * lst[i]
    return result
```

The range function provides the numbers from 1 up to the length of the list minus one, so if we call product(lst), the result will be the product of all the numbers in lst.

```python
lst = [1, 2, 3, 4, 5]
print(product(lst)) # prints 120
```

Note: We use the variable name lst because, if we used the name list, that would override Python's list function.

To find the sum of squares of all the numbers in a list, we could copy the product function, change the name to sum_squares, and replace the fourth line in the function with:

```python
result = result + lst[i] ** 2
```

Unfortunately, this isn't quite correct, because the first element of the list, lst[0], doesn't get squared. To ensure that all the numbers in the list get treated equally, we can include the first value in the range and add a parameter to use as an initial value.

```
def sum_squares(initial, lst):
    result = initial
    for i in range(0, len(lst)):
        result = result + lst[i] ** 2
    return result
```

Now the call sum_squares(0, lst) will work correctly.

To find the sum of all the positive numbers in the list, we could change the name to sum_positives and replace the fourth line with:

```
result = result + max(0, lst[i])
```

All of these functions have essentially identical structure, and it gets tiresome to write the same code over and over again. We have already generalized the function by adding an initial value; let's generalize it further by providing a function to tell it how to combine two elements. We'll name this more general function fold.

```
def fold(initial, fun, lst):
    result = initial
    for i in range(0, len(lst)):
        result = fun(result, lst[i])
    return result
```

Let's define some functions to use with fold:

```
def multiply(a, b):
    return  a  *  b

def count_if_odd(a, b):
    return a + b % 2
```

```
def count_if_prime(a, b):
    if prime(b):
        return a + 1
    else:
        return a

def longer(a, b):
    if len(a) > len(b):
        return a
    else:
        return b
```

Now we no longer have to write a loop to go through a list making pairwise comparisons; instead, we can call the fold function.

```
print(fold(1, multiply, lst)) # prints 120
print(fold(0, count_if_odd, lst))  # prints 3
print(fold(0, count_if_prime, lst))   # prints 3

languages = ['Python', 'Java', 'Scala']
print(fold(", longer, languages))
    # prints 'Python'
```

We can use the fold function in all these different ways because the structure of the code used to combine all the elements is identical; it just differs in the function used to combine a single pair of elements.

To do the above, we had to write additional functions, one for each new thing we wanted fold to do. Unless these functions are needed elsewhere, our code could be improved by using function literals.

```
print(fold(1, lambda a, b: a * b, lst))
print(fold(0, lambda a, b: a + b % 2, lst))
```

And similarly for the others.

3.2 HIGHER-ORDER FUNCTIONS IN JAVA

We can define an integer array as follows:

```
int[] ary = {1, 2, 3, 4, 5};
```

To sum up the numbers in this array, we could do it in Java like this:

```
public static int addAll(int[] ary) {
    int result = ary[0];
    for (int i = 1; i < ary.length; i++) {
        result += ary[i];
    }
    return result;
}

System.out.println(addAll(ary));
```

We could write almost identical methods to find the product of all the numbers in an array, to find the largest or smallest value in an array, and so on. This is a lot of code.

In Section 2.1.2, we defined a function plus, of type IntBinaryOperator, in the class FP. We can now write a reduce function that takes a parameter of this type to tell it how to combine two values.

```
public static int reduce(
        IntBinaryOperator fun, int[] ary) {
    int result = ary[0];
    for (int i = 1; i < ary.length; i++) {
        result = fun.applyAsInt(result, ary[i]);
    }
    return result;
}
```

In Java, methods must be defined within a class. Since we are already assuming the existence of a class named FP, let's add the following methods to that class.

```
public static int multiply(int a, int b) {
    return a * b;
}

public static int lesser(int a, int b) {
    return a < b ? a : b;
}

public static int greater(int a, int b) {
    return a > b ? a : b;
}
```

We can use the :: operator to convert these methods to functions and then pass them to the reduce method like this:

```
System.out.println(reduce(FP::plus, ary));
System.out.println(reduce(FP::multiply, ary));
System.out.println(reduce(FP::lesser, ary));
System.out.println(reduce(FP::greater, ary));
```

These statements will print 15, 120, 1, and 5, respectively.

With function literals, we can bypass methods and go straight to functions.

```
System.out.println(
    reduce((a, b) -> a + b, ary));

System.out.println(
    reduce((a, b) -> a * b, ary));

System.out.println(
    reduce((a, b) -> a < b ? a : b, ary));

System.out.println(
    reduce((a, b) -> a > b ? a : b, ary));
```

In every case, we are going through an array and combining elements pairwise; the only difference is how we combine two elements (by addition, multiplication, or choice).

3.3 HIGHER-ORDER FUNCTIONS IN SCALA

In Scala, we can define a singly linked list like this:

```
val list = List(1, 2, 3, 4, 5)
```

We could find the sum of all the integers in this list by setting up a loop and iterating through the list, referring to each element by its index. Iteration is efficient for arrays but not at all efficient for lists. For lists, recursion is much more efficient.

A list is either *empty* or it isn't. If it isn't empty, it has a *head* (a first element) and a *tail* (the rest of the list after the head). If there is only one element in the list, the head is that one element, and the tail is empty.

With this understanding of lists, we can sum up the elements of a list like this:

```
def addAll(list: List[Int]): Int =
  if (list.tail isEmpty) list.head
  else list.head + addAll(list.tail)

println(addAll(list)) // prints 15
```

Explanation:

- We begin by defining a method called addAll which takes as its one parameter a list of integers and returns an integer result.

- If the list contains only one value, then the tail of the list will be empty (list.tail isEmpty), so we return the head of the list, and we are done. Since there is only the one value in the list, that value is also the sum.

- This code will fail if given an empty list, because an empty list has neither a head nor a tail. We will ignore this issue for the present.

- If the list has more than one value, we can find the sum of all the elements by adding the first element to the sum of the remaining elements.

If we want to find the product of all the elements of a list, or to find the least or greatest value in a list, we could write very similar methods to do these things. Alternatively, we could generalize the above method. All we need to do is to pass in a function as an additional parameter and use that function instead of addition.

Scala requires that we specify the type of every parameter. In this case, we want to pass in a function that takes two integers as parameters and produces an integer as a result. We write this type as (Int, Int) => Int.

Here is the generalized method:

```
def reduce(fun: (Int, Int) => Int,
        list: List[Int]): Int =
    if (list.tail isEmpty) list head
    else fun(list.head, reduce(fun, list tail))
```

And here are some examples of using that method:

```
def add(a: Int, b: Int) = a + b
def multiply(a: Int, b: Int) = a * b
def lesser(a: Int, b: Int) = if (a < b) a else b
def greater(a: Int, b: Int) = if (a > b) a else b

println(reduce(add, list))
println(reduce(multiply, list))
println(reduce(lesser, list))
println(reduce(greater, list))
```

These calls print 15, 120, 1, and 5, respectively.

We can instead use function literals. The code is a bit shorter and does not define otherwise unwanted methods.

```
println(reduce((a: Int, b: Int) => a + b, list))

println(reduce((a: Int, b: Int) => a * b, list))

println(reduce((a: Int, b: Int) =>
          if (a < b) a else b, list))

println(reduce((a: Int, b: Int) =>
          if (a > b) a else b, list))
```

## CHAPTER 4

Functional Interfaces in Java

Uɴʟɪᴋᴇ ᴛʜᴇ ᴏᴛʜᴇʀ ᴄʜᴀᴘᴛᴇʀs, this one is unique to Java; there is no Python or Scala counterpart because those languages had no need of functional interfaces.

Before Java 8, Java had no functions, but it had a lot of classes and a *lot* of methods. These methods weren't compatible with functions. However, many of these classes implemented *interfaces*, and many that didn't could easily be retrofitted to implement interfaces.

As a way of making this older code compatible with functions, Java 8 introduced *functional interfaces*.

4.1 SINGLE ABSTRACT METHODS

In Java, an *interface* is a list of *abstract* (unimplemented) *methods*, possibly along with some other things. A class can *implement* an interface by supplying definitions for those methods.

DOI: 10.1201/9781003358541-4

If an interface lists several abstract methods, all of them must be defined before the interface can be used. However, if the interface lists exactly one **SAM** (**Single Abstract Method**), only that one method must be defined. If we invoke the interface and supply a single function, Java will understand that the function is taking the place of that one method. For this reason, any interface with exactly one SAM is called a *functional interface*.

The function we supply must have the same number and types of parameters as the method it is replacing. Since Java knows the parameter types required by that method, we don't need to specify them in our function.

For example, the `ActionListener` interface has one SAM, `actionPerformed`, which requires an `ActionEvent` as an argument. Since `ActionListener` is a functional interface, we can replace the `actionPerformed` method with a function definition, and we don't need to say that the function parameter has type `ActionEvent`.

```
ActionListener listener = event -> {…}
```

Some familiar interfaces that can be treated as functional interfaces include java.lang.Runnable with a run() method and java.util.Comparator with a compare(*T obj1*, *T obj2*) method.

> **Note:** Although the documentation for `Comparator` lists another abstract method, equals(Object *obj*), that method doesn't have to be implemented in `Comparator`, because `Comparator` can inherit an implementation of equals from `Object`.

4.2 ANONYMOUS INNER CLASSES

Java has a number of interfaces that can be implemented as anonymous inner classes. To respond to a button click in a user interface, we would typically implement java.awt.event.ActionListener as an inner class attached to a button. Here's the original way of doing this:

```
myButton.addActionListener(new ActionListener() {
    @Override
    public void actionPerformed(ActionEvent e) {
        HandleButtonClick();
}});
```

In Java 8, we still need to call addActionListener, but we can skip over creating the ActionListener object and just supply a function for the actionPerformed method.

```
myButton.addActionListener(
    (ActionEvent e) -> {
        HandleButtonClick();
});
```

The resultant code is more direct and slightly less verbose.

A minor variation on this is to define the ActionListener separately, as a function:

```
ActionListener listener = e -> {
    HandleButtonClick();
};
myButton.addActionListener(listener);
```

In this case, the compiler is able to infer the type of e, namely, ActionEvent.

4.3 DEFINING FUNCTIONAL INTERFACES

Any existing functional interface can be used as a type, or you can define your own. For example,

```
@FunctionalInterface
public interface Diddler {
    public abstract int diddle(int x);
}
```

Diddler can be used like this:

```
Diddler y = x -> 3 * x + 1;
System.out.println(y.diddle(5)); // prints 16
```

Here's a slightly more complex example, using type parameters:

```
@FunctionalInterface
public interface Fun2<A, B, R> {
    public R apply(A a, B b);
}
```

Here's an example of using Fun2:

```
Fun2<Integer, Integer, Integer> fn =
    (Integer a, Integer b) -> a % b;
System.out.println(fn.apply(20, 7)); // prints 6
```

4.4 METHOD REFERENCES

Java has tens of thousands of methods, but methods aren't functions. The **method reference operator**, ::, is a way of "wrapping" a method inside a functional interface, so that it can be used as if it were a function.

Essentially, $x :: m$ is an abbreviation of $x \rightarrow x.m(\ldots)$, where m has an unspecified number of parameters. If there is more than one method named m, method resolution is performed in the usual way, by the types and number of parameters.

Here are examples of method reference operators. Explanations are after the code.

```java
import java.util.function.*;

public class MetRef {

    public static void applyTo10(
            IntUnaryOperator intOp) {  // 1
        int result = intOp.applyAsInt(10); // 2
        System.out.println(result);
    }

    public static int square(int x) {
        return x * x;
    }

    public int cube(int x) {
        return x * x * x;
    }

    public static void main(final String[] args) {

        // Using a lambda
        applyTo10(x -> x / 2);        // 3

        // Using a static method
        applyTo10(MetRef :: square); // 4

        // Using a constructor
        Supplier<MetRef> ms = MetRef :: new; // 5
        MetRef m = ms.get();                 // 6
        System.out.println(m.getClass());    // 7

        // Using an instance method
        applyTo10(m :: cube);        // 8
    }
}
```

Explanations:

1. `applyTo10` is a static function that takes one parameter, `intOp`, of type `IntUnaryOperator`. An `IntUnary Operator` is a functional interface whose SAM takes one integer argument and returns an integer result.

2. `intOp.applyAsInt(10)` takes the parameter `intOp` and calls its SAM `applyAsInt` with the parameter `10`. The following line prints the result.

3. `applyTo10(x -> x / 2)` calls `applyTo10` with a simple lambda; 5 is printed.

4. `applyTo10(MetRef :: square)` calls `applyTo10` with the method `square`, which is a *static* method of class `MetRef`; 100 is printed. (Compare to #8 below.)

5. `MetRef :: new` is the form for calling the *constructor* of the class `MetRef`; notice the use of the keyword `new`. Since this particular constructor takes no argument and returns an object, it must be a **supplied** (see Section 4.6.6); and since the type of object supplied is a `MetRef`, the type must be `Supplier <MetRef>`.

6. The supplier in #5 can supply only one object, the newly constructed `MetRef`. We use the supplier's get method to retrieve it.

7. We print the type of the object retrieved in #6. As expected, it prints class `MetRef`.

8. `cube` is an *instance* method, so you can only apply it if you have an instance. We created an instance m in #5 and #6 above. Here, we use `m :: cube` to reference the instance method, just as we used `MetRef :: square` in #4 to reference the static method. The result, `1000`, is printed.

4.5 THE OTHER METHOD REFERENCE

There is a fourth kind of method reference in which we specify a particular instance (object) and the instance method we wish to use, but do not supply the parameters until later. The syntax for this is simply ***instance::method***.

As a first example, suppose we have a class Person with instance variables name and age, a setter method for age, and an instance variable bob of type Person. (We omit the code for this class because it is so routine.) We can create a functional interface to change Bob's age like this:

```
Consumer<Integer> g = bob::setAge;
```

We can use method g like this:

```
g.accept(44);
```

The setAge method is defined as public void setAge(int age). Because it returns nothing (void), the corresponding functional interface must be a Consumer. Because its single argument is an int, the type of functional interface must be Consumer<Integer>. Finally, this functional interface has a single abstract method, accept.

As a second example, the String class has an instance method indexOf which takes a string to search for in the given instance and returns the index at which it is found. That is,

```
System.out.println("computer".indexOf("t"));
```

will print 5. Comparable code to do the same thing is:

```
String s = "computer";
Function<String, Integer> find = s::indexOf;
System.out.println(find.apply("t"));
```

The parameters and return type of indexOf require the use of a Function<String, Integer> with the single abstract method apply.

4.6 PROVIDED FUNCTIONAL INTERFACES

In addition to the interfaces that are functional by default because they have only one single abstract method, Java provides 43 new predefined functional interfaces. In this section, I have tried to organize those functional interfaces in as memorable a fashion as I can and provide some useful mnemonics.

Frankly, these interfaces are unnecessary. They are more efficient than any interfaces you can write but add no functionality. The previous sections showed how you can define your own functional interfaces. If you are reading this book simply to get an understanding of functional programming, you can skip ahead to Section 5, *If Expressions*, or you can quickly skim this list of predefined functional operators.

To use these functional interfaces, import java.util.function.*.

4.6.1 IntPredicate

In this section, we take an in-depth look at one functional interface.

The interface IntPredicate has boolean test(int *value*) as its SAM (Single Abstract Method). Here is an example of its use:

```
IntPredicate even = n -> n % 2 == 0;
System.out.println(even.test(3)); // prints false
```

The first thing to notice is that IntPredicate takes no type parameters; its SAM takes an integer and returns a boolean.

There is a more general interface, Predicate<*T*>, which takes a type parameter *T*; its SAM takes a parameter of type *T* and returns a boolean. It can be used almost exactly the same way as IntPredicate, but it is much slower, because the int argument n must be boxed into an Integer.

```
Predicate<Integer> even2 = n -> n % 2 == 0;
System.out.println(even2.test(3)); // prints false
```

Java makes a distinction between **primitives** and **objects**. Primitives are simple values: int, double, long, and boolean, to name the most common kinds. However, **type parameters** (such as *T* above) *must be object types*; they cannot be primitives. To deal with this, Java introduced **wrapper classes**, that is, classes whose purpose is to hold a single primitive value. An Integer is a wrapper that holds a single int, Boolean holds a single boolean, and so on. So, while we cannot say Predicate<int>, we *can* say Predicate<Integer>.

Sometime later, Java introduced automatic wrapping and unwrapping, so that the user could use, for example, an int where an Integer was required (as n in the even2 example above), and the compiler would quietly create the necessary object. (However, primitive types still can't be used as type parameters.)

Wrapping and unwrapping is inefficient. IntPredicate takes a primitive int as an argument; this means it can't take any other kind of argument, but it can be much more efficient. About half the provided functional interfaces are present simply to avoid wrapping and unwrapping.

4.6.2 Function Composition

While a functional interface must have exactly one *abstract* method, Java 8 allows interfaces to also have **static** methods and **default** methods (as specified using the static and default keywords). A primary distinction between these is that default methods may be overridden, while static methods cannot be overridden.

The IntPredicate interface has, in addition to its abstract test method, the following default methods:

- default IntPredicate and(IntPredicate *other*)

- default IntPredicate or(IntPredicate *other*)

- default IntPredicate negate()

Values can be combined in various ways (addition, etc.) to form new values. In an functional language, functions are values, so there should be some way of combining functions to form new functions. One of these ways is *function composition*. The above default methods allow us to compose abstract methods from the IntPredicate interface.

The and and or methods are *short-circuit methods*. For and, if the first method evaluates to false, the second method need not be evaluated; the result must be false. For or, if the first method evaluates to true, the second method need not be evaluated; the result must be true. We can demonstrate this by writing a couple of functions that include print statements.

```
IntPredicate big = n ->
  { System.out.print("big ");
    return n > 1000; };

IntPredicate even = n ->
  { System.out.print("even ");
    return n % 2 == 0; };

IntPredicate bigEven = big.and(even);
```

```
System.out.println(bigEven.test(6));
// prints: big false

System.out.println(bigEven.test(6000));
// prints: big even true

System.out.println(big.or(even).test(1001));
// prints: big true
```

Above, we used the and method to compose big and even to create a new method, which we then assigned to the variable bigEven (of type IntPredicate).

In the last print statement above, we did something a little different. We used the or method to compose big and even, but rather than giving the resultant function a name, we used it directly.

The third method, negate, negates its argument:

```
System.out.println(even.negate().test(5));
// prints: even true

IntPredicate odd = even.negate();
System.out.println(odd.test(5)); // prints: even true
```

> **Note**: The above call to odd prints, somewhat confusingly, the word even. This is because odd calls even, which prints its name. It is generally poor style to do both computation and input/output in a single function.

4.6.3 Predicates Again

As we have seen, Predicate<*T*> is a functional interface with a SAM (Single Abstract Method), boolean test(*T t*). Table 4.1 lists all the predicates along with their SAMs.

TABLE 4.1   The predicates and their SAMs

Interface	Single Abstract Method
Predicate<*T*>	boolean test(T *t*)
DoublePredicate	boolean test(double *value*)
IntPredicate	boolean test(int *value*)
LongPredicate	boolean test(long *value*)
BiPredicate<*T*, *U*>	boolean test(T*t*, *U u*)

Most of these have no type parameters because none are needed. All of them have the default methods and, or, and negate.

4.6.4 Unary Operators

As the name implies, unary operators apply to a single argument. There are four functional interfaces defined by Java 8, and each of them returns a result of the same type as its argument; they are listed in Table 4.2.

Each of these has two default methods and one static method. The default methods are:

- *f*.andThen(*g*): Returns a function that applies *f* to its argument and then applies *g* to that result.

- *f*.compose(*g*): Returns a function that applies *g* to its argument and then applies *f* to that result.

TABLE 4.2   Unary operators and their SAMs

Interface	Single Abstract Method
DoubleUnaryOperator	double applyAsDouble(double *operand*)
IntUnaryOperator	int applyAsInt(int *operand*)
LongUnaryOperator	long applyAsLong (long *operand*)
UnaryOperator<*T*>	*T* apply(*T operand*)

The default methods take a parameter of the same type as the interface and produce the same type as a result. That is, the default methods for DoubleUnaryOperator take a DoubleUnaryOperator as a parameter and produce a DoubleUnaryOperator result, and similarly for each of the other unary operators.

The single static method is identity(), which always returns the argument given to it. For example, IntUnaryOperator.identity().applyAsInt(77) returns 77.

4.6.5 More Functions and Operators

The most general functional interfaces and their SAMs (single abstract methods) are given in Table 4.3.

TABLE 4.3   Functional interfaces and their SAMs

Interface	Single Abstract Method
Function<T, R>	R apply($T\,t$)
BiFunction<T, U, R>	R apply($T\,t$, $U\,u$)
BinaryOperator<T>	T apply($T\,t1$, $T\,t2$)

A number of the remaining functional interfaces are named using the word Function or Operator. They are hard to group in any meaningful manner. However, the names tell a lot about them.

- If the name contains Bi or Binary, its SAM takes two parameters; otherwise, its SAM takes a single parameter.

- If the name starts with Double, Int, or Long, and is not a Supplier, then its SAM takes parameters of that type. (Suppliers take no arguments.)

- If the name contains To, for example, DoubleToInt, then its SAM returns the primitive type after To (an int).

- If the name begins with ToDouble, ToInt, or ToLong, then its SAM takes parameterized types (<*T t*> or [if the name also includes Bi] <*T t, U u*>) as parameters and returns the named type.

- If the name ends in Operator, its SAM returns the same type as its arguments; but if the name ends in Function, then it returns a parameterized type.

- If a functional interface has double, int, or long as its return type, its SAM is named applyAsDouble, applyAsInt, or applyAsLong, respectively. Otherwise, its SAM is named apply.

The above rules do not apply to suppliers, consumers, or predicates. Table 4.4 lists the functional interfaces to which it *does* apply.

TABLE 4.4 Usefully named interfaces

BiFunction	LongBinaryOperator
BinaryOperator	LongFunction
DoubleBinaryOperator	LongToDoubleFunction
DoubleFunction	LongToIntFunction
DoubleToIntFunction	LongUnaryOperator
DoubleToLongFunction	ToDoubleBiFunction
DoubleUnaryOperator	ToDoubleFunction
Function	ToIntBiFunction
IntBinaryOperator	ToIntFunction
IntFunction	ToLongBiFunction
IntToDoubleFunction	ToLongFunction
IntToLongFunction	UnaryOperator
IntUnaryOperator	

4.6.6 Suppliers and Consumers

A **supplier** is a function that takes no arguments but returns some value. It may read data from a file or return the time or a random number.

TABLE 4.5   Suppliers

Interface	Single Abstract Method
Supplier<*T*>	*T* get()
BooleanSupplier	boolean getAsBoolean()
DoubleSupplier	double getAsDouble()
IntSupplier	int getAsInt()
LongSupplier	long getAsLong()

A *consumer* is a function that takes an argument, does something with it, and returns void. For example, the argument may be logged, printed, or saved to a file.

TABLE 4.6   Consumers

Interface	Single Abstract Method
Consumer<*T*>	void accept(*T t*)
BiConsumer<*T, U*>	void accept(*T t, U u*)
DoubleConsumer	void accept(double *value*)
IntConsumer	void accept(int *value*)
LongConsumer	void accept(long *value*)
ObjDoubleConsumer<*T*>	void accept(*T t*, double *value*)
ObjIntConsumer<*T*>	void accept(*T t*, int *value*)
ObjLongConsumer<*T*>	void accept(*T t*, long *value*)

As no new concepts are involved, the supplier functional interfaces and their SAMs are listed in Table 4.5, and the consumer functional interfaces and their SAMs are listed in Table 4.6.

The first five consumer methods, Consumer through LongConsumer, also have a default andThen method.

## CHAPTER 5

If Expressions

A N *IF STATEMENT* CHOOSES which of several statements to execute, but an *if expression* chooses which of several expressions to evaluate. The value of the chosen expression is the value of the if expression.

If expressions are not unique to functional programming, but they add considerably to the range of things a function literal can do while keeping it reasonably concise. Also, functional languages tend to be expression oriented, so they require if expressions. For these reasons, a brief review of if expressions is in order.

5.1 IF EXPRESSIONS IN PYTHON

The body of a literal function must be a single expression. Python's *if expression* extends the range of what can be done in that expression. The syntax is:

> *value1* if *condition* else *value2*

DOI: 10.1201/9781003358541-5

The *condition* is evaluated, and if true, *value1* is computed and returned; but if false, *value2* is computed and returned.

We can use if expressions to find the least and greatest values in a list:

```
least =
    fold(lst[0], lambda a, b: a if a < b else b, lst)

greatest =
    fold(lst[0], lambda a, b: a if a > b else b, lst)
```

If you remember how the fold function works its way down a list, starting with the first element and combining each value with the next value in the list, the above is neither difficult to understand nor difficult to read.

5.2 IF EXPRESSIONS IN JAVA

Java has the so-called *ternary expression*, with the syntax

> *condition* ? *valueIfTrue* : *valueIfFalse*

The type and the value of this expression both depend on the condition. If the condition is true, the value of the expression is *valueIfTrue*, with the corresponding type; if the condition is false, the value of the expression is *valueIfFalse*, and the type is the type of that expression.

The ternary expression can only be used in a context where either type is acceptable. For example, the following assignment is legal:

```
Object ternary = true ? 123 : "abc";
```

The following is not legal:

```
int ternary = true ? 123 : "abc";
```

If you combine two or more ternary expressions, it is a good idea to use parentheses to make the code more readable.

```
int score = s < 0 ? 0 : (s > 100 ? 100 : s);
```

5.3 IF EXPRESSIONS IN SCALA

An if expression:

- begins with if (*condition*) *expression*,

- has any number of else if (*condition*) *expression* clauses, and

- ends with an optional else *expression*.

The value of the if expression is the value of the first expression whose condition evaluates to true.

```
val a = 5
val b = 8.0
val max = if (a > b) a else b
```

Since a is not greater than b, the second expression, b, is evaluated and assigned to the variable max.

The type of the result is always a type that can hold any value chosen. In the above example, a is an Int and b is a Double; either value can be assigned to a Double, but 8.0 cannot be assigned to an Int, so the result must be of type Double, regardless of which value is chosen.

In most functional languages, an if expression must have an else part, because an expression has to have some value. Scala, however, allows the else part to be omitted. If no expression is chosen and there is no else clause, the result will be (), which is the special "unit" value. This affects the return type of the if expression.

If an expression has no else clause, then:

- If every expression results in a number, a boolean, or the unit value, the result will be of type AnyVal.

- If any expression results in any other type of object, the result will be of type Any.

Comprehensions

A **COMPREHENSION** IS A CONCISE way to construct a new sequence of values, based on a sequence that has already been defined. For example, given a list of numbers, we might construct a list of the squares of those numbers.

One of the principles of functional programming is that data values are, or should be, immutable. In an imperative program, one might loop through an array and square each element, thus mutating the array. Comprehensions are more functional because they apply a transformation to each element and return the transformed sequence, but do not modify the original sequence.

In functional programming, the list is the most commonly used type of sequence, but there may be comprehensions for other types as well.

DOI: 10.1201/9781003358541-6

6.1 LIST COMPREHENSIONS IN PYTHON

Python has four kinds of *comprehensions*: list, set, dictionary, and generator comprehensions. We will go into detail only with list comprehensions; the others are very similar.

A list comprehension looks like this:

> [*expression* for *variable* in *list* if *condition*]

A list comprehension computes a new list based on an existing list. It steps through the *list*, puts each value from the list into the *variable*, tests the *condition*, and if the condition is satisfied, computes the *expression* and puts it into the new list. The test part (if *condition*) can be omitted, in which case every value in *list* is used in creating the new list.

Typically, both the *condition* and the *expression* use the *variable*, but this is not a requirement.

Here are some examples, along with the values they produce. Assume in each case that nums is the list [1, 2, 3, 4, 5].

```
[10 * x for x in nums if x < 4]
# Result is [10, 20, 30]

[1 for x in nums if even(x)]
# Result is [1, 1]

[x * x for x in nums]
# Result is [1, 4, 9, 16, 25]

[v for v in "functional" if v in "aeiou"]
# Result is ['u', 'i', 'o', 'a']
```

The last example uses the fact that Python can treat a string as a list of letters.

A list comprehension can be used wherever a list can be used.

```
print([x * x for x in
    [2 * y for y in range(1, 5)]])
# Prints [4, 16, 36, 64]
```

You can even combine if expressions with list comprehensions.

```
for n in [x // 2 if x % 2 == 0
                else 3 * x + 1
            for x in range(1, 5)]:
    print(n)
# Prints four lines: 4, 1, 10, 2
```

Note: In Python, // is integer division.

A *set* is a data structure in which there are no duplicate values, and for which the order of values is irrelevant.

A *set comprehension* looks just like a list comprehension, except that it is enclosed in braces, {}, rather than brackets, [].

```
{c.upper() for c in "bookkeeper" if c in "aeiou"}
# Result is {'E', 'O'}
```

A *dictionary* is a number of *key:value* pairs, enclosed in braces.

```
d = {'one': 1, 'two': 2, 'three':3, 'four':4}
```

A *dictionary comprehension* will step through the keys.

```
{key:d[key] for key in d if key[0] == 't'}
# Result is {'two': 2, 'three': 3}
```

A *generator comprehension* looks like a list comprehension, except that it uses parentheses, ( ), instead of brackets, [ ]. The difference is that the generator is an object that produces values one at a time when its next() method is called. If there are no more values, an exception is raised.

Generator comprehensions can be used in for loops; the loop handles the exception.

```
for e in (x * x for x in [1, 2, 3]):
    print(e)
# Prints 1, 4, and 9
```

There is no way to determine in advance whether the generator has any additional values.

6.2 COMPREHENSIONS IN JAVA

Java does not have comprehensions.

6.3 FOR EXPRESSIONS IN SCALA

Scala's for comprehensions are based on *for expressions* and will be covered in the next section.

A for expression, when used as a statement for its side effects, has the syntax

```
for (sequence) expression
```

In this form, the value returned is always the Unit value, ().

The *sequence* can be quite complex. It always starts with a *generator* (indicated by the <- arrow) to provide a sequence of values. In the following examples, the comment (after //) shows what is printed, with each value on a separate line.

```
for (e <- List(2, 3, 5, 7)) println(e)
// prints 2, 3, 5, 7

for (e <- 1 to 5) println(e)
// prints 1, 2, 3, 4, 5

for (e <- 1 until 5) println(e)
// prints 1, 2, 3, 4

for (e <- 1 to 10 by 3) println(e)
// prints 1, 4, 7, 10

for (e <- List.range(1, 5)) println(e)
// prints 1, 2, 3, 4

for (e <- List.range(1, 10, 3)) println(e)
// prints 1, 4, 7

for (e <- "abc") println(e)
// prints a, b, c
```

There can be more than one generator. For example, the following will print out, in 81 lines, a crude multiplication table:

```
for (i <- 2 to 10;
     j <- 2 to 10)
  println(i + "*" + j + "=" + i * j)
```

The initial generator may be followed by additional generators, definitions, and filters.

- A *definition* has the form *variable* = *expression* (the keywords var and val are not used here). Variables defined in this way are local to the for expression; they are not available afterward.

- A *filter* has the form if *condition*. If the condition is false, the currently generated value is discarded, and computation continues with the next generated value (if any).

Examples:

```
for (e <- 1 to 6;
     if e != 4)
  println(e)        // prints 1, 2, 3, 5, 6

// print the same multiplication table as before
for (i <- 2 to 10;
     j <- 2 to 10;
     ij = i * j)
  println(i + "*" + j + "=" + ij)

for (e <- "computer";
     v <- "aeiou";
     if e == v)
  println(e)        // prints o, u, e

for (v <- "aeiou";
     e <- "computer";
     if e == v)
  println(e)        // prints e, o, u

val n = 100
for (e <- 2 to Math.sqrt(n).toInt;
     if n % e == 0)
  println(e)        // prints 2, 4, 5, 10

// print all 2-digit numbers containing 7
for (n <- 10 to 100;
     s = n.toString();
     if s contains '7')
  println(n)
```

6.4 FOR COMPREHENSIONS IN SCALA

A *for comprehension* has the syntax

```
for (sequence) yield expression
```

Just as in the case of a for expression without a yield, the *sequence* begins with a generator and may contain any number of generators, definitions, and filters. Variables defined in the *sequence* may be used (with their current values) in the *expression*.

A for comprehension is used for its value, so usually that value is assigned to a variable.

Examples:

```
val a = for (e <- 1 to 6;
        if e != 4
      ) yield e
// sets a to Vector(1, 2, 3, 5, 6)

val n = 50
val b = for (e <- 2 to n;
        if n % e == 0
      ) yield e
// sets b to Vector(2, 5, 10, 25, 50)

val c = for (e <- "computer";
        if "aeiou" contains e
      ) yield e
// sets c to the string "oue"
```

Suppose we wish to find all 5-digit numbers that (a) are palindromes and (b) whose sum of digits is 20. This can be done with a single for comprehension, assigning the result to the variable p.

```
val p = for (
        n <- 10000 to 99999;
        s1 = n toString();
        s2 = s1 reverse;
        if s1 == s2;
        d = for (x <- s1) yield x asDigit;
        sum = d.sum
        if sum == 20
      ) yield n
```

The value this assigns to p is List(15851, 16661, 17471, ..., 91019).

The same computation can be made in an imperative way, using loops and assignment statements, but the code is harder to read and understand.

```
var p: List[Int] = List()
for (n <- 10000 to 99999) {
  var s1 = n toString;
  var s2 = s1 reverse;
  if (s1 == s2) {
    var sum = 0
    for (x <- s1) {
      sum += x.asDigit
    }
    if (sum == 20) {
      p = p :+ n
    }
  }
}
```

## CHAPTER 7

Closures

I DEALLY, A FUNCTION SHOULD be **pure**: it should take no information from the environment in which it is defined. An **impure function** is one that uses values in its environment.

Because a function is a value, it can be put in a variable and that variable can be transported a long way from where the function was defined. The environment in which the function was defined may no longer exist, and the storage that environment used for variables may have been garbage collected. If the function is impure—if it uses variables from that environment—they may now have garbage values. Obviously, this is undesirable.

A **closure** is a way to prevent this from happening, by "closing over" any such external values and carrying them along with the function. How this is implemented is not important; what is important is that the programmer does not have to be concerned with whether the function still works.

DOI: 10.1201/9781003358541-7

7.1 CLOSURES IN PYTHON

Consider the following code:

```
x = 1
def my_closure(y):
    return lambda z: x + y + z
```

In this function,

- x is not a local variable of my_closure but is defined outside the function.

- y is considered to be a local variable because it is a parameter.

- my_closure returns a function which takes a parameter z.

- When called, the returned function will compute the sum x + y + z.

Now, we call my_closure and save the returned function in a variable c:

```
c = my_closure(10)
```

Finally, we call the returned function (now in c) with the argument 100 and print the result:

```
print('c(100) is', c(100))
# prints: c(100) is 111
```

$(x = 1, y = 10,$ and $z = 100,$ so their sum is 111$)$.

Under ordinary circumstances, local variables of a function (including parameters such as y) are deleted and the memory they use is recycled when the function returns. That didn't happen here.

The function my_closure returned a function which was assigned to c. This function contained a reference to local variable y, which the function defined by lambda has "captured," or "closed over," so that it wasn't deleted. (This would work equally well if the inner function were defined by def rather than by lambda.)

Changes to the global variable x and the parameter z have the results that should be expected:

```
x = 5
print('c(200) is', c(200))
# prints: c(200) is 215
```

The external variable x has been changed to 5; the parameter z of the function now named c is set to 200, but the function c was created with 10 as the value of its parameter y, and that value has been retained.

7.2 CLOSURES IN JAVA

In Java, a method cannot be defined within another method, but a function can be defined within a method (or within another function).

As a simple example, suppose we want to write a function that simply adds 10 to its argument. The function itself can be written as,

```
(x) -> x + 10
```

Now, let's write a method that returns this function. To do this, we have to figure out the type of the function. Since it takes an int as a parameter and returns an int as a value, the type has to be IntUnaryOperator.

```
IntUnaryOperator add10() {
    return (x) -> x + 10;
}
```

The SAM (Single Abstract Method) defined for IntUnary-Operator is applyAsInt; therefore, we can call the function returned by add10 like this:

```
IntUnaryOperator adder = add10();
System.out.println(adder.applyAsInt(5)); // prints 15
```

This isn't yet a closure, as it does not refer to any variables in the enclosing method. We can modify the method and function to get this:

```
IntUnaryOperator addN() {
  int y = 10;
  return (x) -> x + y;
}
```

The function returned by addN can be called in a similar fashion (using applyAsInt) and will produce the same results. This is as close to being a closure as Java gets. However, the following is illegal and will not work:

```
IntUnaryOperator addN() {
  int y = 9;
  y = y + 1;
  return (x) -> x + y;
}
```

The reason this fails is that Java cannot actually close over variables. What it *can* do is close over constants. If a variable is declared to be final, or if it is "effectively final" because it is assigned a value once and never changed, then its value can be used in the function returned by the method.

7.3 CLOSURES IN SCALA

Here is a simple method that takes a parameter x and returns a function that will multiply its parameter by x.

```
def conversion(factor: Double) =
   (x: Int) => factor * x
```

This is an example of a closure. The variable factor is a parameter, so it is a local variable of the conversion method, but it is used in a function that is returned by conversion. The method has "closed over" this variable.

Here, are some examples of using the above method:

```
val inch2cm = conversion(2.54)
val pounds2kg = conversion(0.453592)

print(inch2cm(12))    // Prints 30.48
print(pounds2kg(150)) // Prints 68.0388
```

In the above, the variable being closed over has a fixed value. It is not the value that is being closed over, but the variable itself. In the following code, the remind function closes over the variable date.

```
var date = new Date()

def remind(name: String) =
   "\nDear " + name + ", It is now " + date +
      ",\nand I am writing to remind you …"
```

Each time the remind function is called, it uses the current value of date, not necessarily the value it had at the time the function was defined.

```
println(remind("Jane"))
Thread.sleep(1000) // pause one second
date = new Date()
println(remind("Bill"))
```

Notice that the printed times differ by one second.

```
Dear Jane, It is now Thu Nov 24 16:08:11 EST 2022,
and I am writing to remind you …

Dear Bill, It is now Thu Nov 24 16:08:12 EST 2022,
and I am writing to remind you …
```

7.4 CLOSURE EXAMPLE

A simple cubic polynomial can be written as,

$$ax^3 + bx^2 + cx + d$$

where a, b, c, and d are the coefficients. If we were given the task of graphing several polynomials with different coefficients, we could write a polynomial function that, given the coefficients, returned a function that used those coefficients. We'll use Python for this example; Scala is similar.

```
def polynomial(a, b, c, d):
    return lambda x: (a * x**3 + b * x**2 + c * x + d)

p = polynomial(1, 10, 100, 1000)
print(p(1), p(10)) # prints 1111 4000
```

This works, but we have to call polynomial with a new set of coefficients each time we want to graph another polynomial. A better solution is to close over the coefficients and get a single function that uses the coefficients from the environment.

```
def poly():
    return lambda x: (a * x**3 + b * x**2 + c * x + d)

f = poly()
```

Now, let's test our new function f:

```
a, b, c, d = 1, 10, 100, 1000
print(f(1), f(10)) # prints 1111 4000

a = 0; d = 0
print(f(1), f(10)) # prints 110 2000
```

## CHAPTER 8

Currying

N O DESCRIPTION OF FUNCTIONAL programming would be complete without a mention of *currying*. Currying is a technique developed by the mathematician Haskell Curry (the programming language Haskell is also named after him). *Currying* is a technique to convert a function that takes multiple parameters into a series of functions, each taking a single function.

In the following example, we curry a formula function of four arguments into four functions (named f, g, h, and j), each taking a single argument. The example is in Python because it has simpler syntax than either Java or Scala.

```
def formula(x, a, b, c):
    return (a * x ** 2) + (b * x) + c
```

One way of currying the formula function is as follows:

```
def f(x):
    def g(a):
        def h(b):
```

DOI: 10.1201/9781003358541-8

```
    def j(c):
      return (a * x ** 2) + (b * x) + c
    return j
  return h
return g

print(f(10)(1)(2)(3)) // 1*100 + 2*10 + 3 = 123
```

When function f(10) is called, it returns a function g. Function g is a *closure*; it "closes over" the value of 10 for x, which is used inside function g. When that function is called with the argument 1, the function returned by f(10)(1) has closed over the value 1 for a; and so on. By the time we get to function j, values have been assigned to all of x, a, b, and c, and the expression can be evaluated.

Currying may seem like a mathematical "trick" with little practical value. If we insist on the strict mathematical definition of currying, this is probably true; but we can generalize the concept into something more useful.

> **Generalized definition**: To *curry* a function is to absorb (close over) one or more parameters, yielding a new function with fewer parameters. The absorbed parameters are treated as constants in the new function.

In our (nonmathematical) definition, it doesn't have to be the *first* parameter that is closed over, nor do we have to close over just one parameter.

Currying isn't all that useful if it is used to create just *one* new function. Rather, you should think of currying as a way to build a "factory" that can create a number of similar functions, each with different values of its parameters.

> **Comparison with closures**: The purpose of a *closure* is to capture information from its environment, so that the

function can be used elsewhere. Closures aren't usually versions of an existing function that has more parameters.

The purpose of *currying* is to generate a series of functions as specializations of an existing function. The "internal" functions defined by the curried function are closures because they use information provided by the enclosing function(s), but the outermost function (f in the above example) is usually not a closure.

8.1 CURRYING IN PYTHON

Currying, as generalized in the previous section, is a way to take a function of several arguments and fix, or "bake in," specific values of one or more arguments, so that only the remaining arguments need to be specified. As an example, we will start with the following function:

```
def prefix(before, text):
    return before + text
```

If we want the before parameter to have the value 'Note:', it's easy enough to write a function that calls prefix:

```
def note(text):
    return prefix('Note: ', text)
```

This gives us the desired function, but it isn't currying. If we wanted a series of functions, each with a different value for before, we could make multiple copies of the note function and edit each one to do what we want. Alternatively, we can write a function curry2 that takes prefix as one of its arguments and writes the note function (and some others) for us.

```
def curry2(fun, arg):
    return lambda text: fun(arg, text)
```

```
note = curry2(prefix, 'Note: ')
warn = curry2(prefix, 'Warning! ')
pow2 = curry2(pow, 2)

print(note('Sealed unit.'))
# prints 'Note: Sealed unit.'
print(warn('Live wire!'))
# prints 'Warning! Live wire!'
print(pow2(10))              # prints 1024
```

Currying is most often used to absorb the first parameter into a function. The above curry2 function does this but only for the special case of a function with exactly two arguments. A more general curry function can be written to handle an arbitrary number of arguments.

```
def curry(f, x):
    return lambda *args: f(x, *args)

def formula(x, a, b, c):
    return (a * x ** 2) + (b * x) + c

use_10_for_x = curry(formula, 10)
print(use_10_for_x(1, 2, 3)) # prints 123
```

In the above definition of the curry function, the first asterisk is used to wrap any number of arguments into a list, while the second is used to unwrap that list into discrete arguments.

Again from a mathematical viewpoint, currying absorbs the *first* argument into a function to create a new function. We don't have to be so limited. We can absorb any arguments we like into a new function. For example, sometimes we want to surround some text with braces, sometimes parentheses, sometimes something else.

```
def surround(before, text, after):
    return before + text + after
```

```
def enclose(fun, before, after):
    return lambda text: fun(before, text, after)

parens = enclose(surround, '(', ')')
print(parens('see above')) # prints '(see above)'
```

The enclose function takes a function (surround) as one of its arguments and produces a specialized function as its result. Thus, it is a reasonable example of currying.

If you are comfortable with the idea of a function returning a function, however, you can write a simpler enclose function that doesn't need surround at all.

```
def enclose(before, after):
    return lambda text: before + text + after

parens = enclose('(', ')')
braces = enclose('{ ', ' }')
sic = enclose(", '[sic]')
bold = enclose('<b>', '</b>')

print(parens('see above')) # prints '(see above')
print(braces('1, 2, 3'))   # prints '{ 1, 2, 3 }'
print(sic('nuculear'))     # prints 'nuculear[sic]'
print(bold('now!'))        # prints '<b>now!</b>'
```

8.2 CURRYING IN JAVA

Currying can be done in Java with the traditional syntax. In this example, we will curry a function that multiplies its two parameters to get one that multiplies its one parameter by a constant.

```
public static IntUnaryOperator f1(int x) {
    return new IntUnaryOperator() {
        @Override
        public int applyAsInt(int y) {
```

```
        return x * y;
    }
  };
}
```

Or with the much shorter "lambda" syntax:

```
public static Function<Integer, Integer> f2(int x) {
    return y -> x * y;
}
```

The first of these can be called as,

```
IntUnaryOperator h1 = f1(3);
System.out.println(h1.applyAsInt(7));
```

The second can be called as,

```
Function h2 = f2(3);
System.out.println(h2.apply(7));
```

In both cases, 21 will be printed.

Somewhat more generally, the following can curry a two-parameter integer function into a one-parameter integer function.

```
IntUnaryOperator curry(int x, IntBinaryOperator op) {
    return z -> op.applyAsInt(x, z);
}

IntUnaryOperator add12 = curry(12, simpleAdd);
System.out.println(add12.applyAsInt(4)); // 16
```

8.3 CURRYING IN SCALA

Currying can be done in Scala the same way that it can in Python. For example, we will take a function that adds a prefix to some text and curry it to make a prefix "factory" to create any number of specialized functions.

```
def prefix(pre: String,
          text: String): String = pre + text

def curry2(f: (String, String) => String,
          arg1: String) =
  (arg2: String) => f(arg1, arg2)

  val note = curry2(prefix, "Note: ")
  val caution = curry2(prefix, "Caution: ")

  println(note("Refer to the manual."))
  println(caution("Unplug before opening."))
```

Since Scala is designed to be a functional language, there is a simpler way of doing this. By giving prefix two parameter lists, supplying a value for only the first will return a curried function.

```
def prefix(pre: String)
          (text: String): String = pre + text

val warn = prefix("Warning: ") _
val danger = prefix("Danger! ")("Live wire!")

println(warn("Surface may be hot."))
println(danger)
```

In the definition of warn, a final underscore is necessary to reassure Scala that the lack of an argument list is not an error. Called with one argument list, warn returns a function; called with two, warn returns the resultant string.

A function in Scala may be defined with any number of parameter lists, with any number of parameters in each. Calling such a function with fewer argument lists will return a function that requires the remaining argument lists.

Similar to currying, Scala has ***partially applied functions***. To partially apply a function, simply replace a value or values in the argument list with underscores, along with their types. The result is a function that can later be called with just the missing arguments.

```scala
def formula(x: Int, a: Int, b: Int, c: Int) =
  (a * x * x) + (b * x) + c

println(formula(10, 1, 2, 3)) // prints 123

val f10 = formula(10, _: Int, _:Int, _:Int)
println(f10(4, 5, 6)) // prints 456

val fx = formula(_: Int, 7, 8, 9)
println(fx(10)) // prints 789
```

## CHAPTER 9

Function Composition

FUNCTIONS ARE VALUES, so there should be some way to operate on functions to produce new functions.

Function composition is the simplest of these operations. It takes two functions f and g and produces a new function h such that $h(x) = f(g(x))$.

Function composition is straightforward in almost any programming language. Functional programming languages sometimes provide a more abbreviated syntax for doing this.

9.1 FUNCTION COMPOSITION IN PYTHON

It's quite easy in Python to create new functions from old ones. For example,

```
big = lambda x: x > 1000
even = lambda x: x % 2 == 0

big_even = lambda x: big(x) and even(x)
```

DOI: 10.1201/9781003358541-9

This is very much like writing,

```
def big_even(x):
    return big(x) and even(x)
```

There's nothing much new here; we're just calling functions from within other functions. We can do the same thing in a much more general fashion, by writing a function that takes two functions as arguments and returns a function.

```
andf = lambda f, g: lambda x: f(x) and g(x)
```

This is a bit complicated, so let's take it slow.

1. We're assigning something to andf. The value we are assigning must be a function, since it starts with lambda.

2. The part before the first colon is lambda f, g. The parameters f and g could be any type; but if we look ahead, we see f(x) and g(x), so f and g must be functions.

3. The part *after* the first colon is supposed to be the value returned by the function; but what is it? Well, it starts with lambda, so the value to be returned must also be a function.

4. The value being returned is therefore lambda x: f(x) and g(x). This is a function that takes one argument, x, and does something with it. Specifically, it calls the functions f and g and combines the results using and.

Now, let's try it.

```
big_even_2 = andf(big, even)

big_even_2(5)    # Result is False
big_even_2(5000) # Result is True
big_even_2(9999) # Result is False
```

9.2 FUNCTION COMPOSITION IN JAVA

Java has two methods for composing functions: andThen and compose. These can be found in the Function interface in java. util.function.

> *function1*.andThen(*function2*) returns a function. This new function applies *function1* to the parameter and then applies *function2* to the result.

> *function1*.compose(*function2*) returns a function. This new function applies *function2* to the parameter and then applies *function1* to the result.

Examples:

```
IntUnaryOperator triple = x -> 3 * x;
IntUnaryOperator square = x -> x * x;
IntUnaryOperator tripleThenSquare =
    triple.andThen(square);
IntUnaryOperator squareAfterTripling =
    triple.compose(square);

System.out.println(tripleThenSquare
            .applyAsInt(5));
// Prints 225

System.out.println(squareAfterTripling
            .applyAsInt(5));
// Prints 75
```

There are a number of limitations. For example, consider the following function:

```
IntBinaryOperator larger =
    (x, y) -> x > y ? x : y;
```

Even though this function produces a single integer result, an IntBinaryOperator has no andThen method. Consequently, larger.andThen(square) is illegal.

9.3 FUNCTION COMPOSITION IN SCALA

In Scala, andThen is a binary operator that composes two functions. It creates a new function in which the result of calling the left
function is the value passed as an argument to the right function.
This is best explained by example.

In the following paragraphs, we first define a method adjust and
a function passing. Since adjust is a method, it will need to be
converted to a function before it can be used with andThen.

```scala
def adjust(score: Int) =
  if (score < 0) 0
  else if (score > 100) 100
  else score

val passing = (score: Int) => score >= 70
```

The method adjust takes an integer parameter and returns an
integer result. The function passing determines whether its argument is greater than or equal to 70.

To convert adjust to a function, we use the postfix operator _ (an
underscore) like this: adjust _.

We now have two functions that we can compose using andThen.
The resultant function, eval, takes one integer argument, calls
adjust with that integer, and then calls passing with the result.

```scala
val eval = adjust _ andThen passing
```

Now, we can use the eval function.

```scala
println(eval(69)) // Prints false
println(eval(70)) // Prints true
```

## CHAPTER 10

Optional Values

Tᴏɴʏ Hᴏᴀʀᴇ ɪɴᴠᴇɴᴛᴇᴅ ᴛʜᴇ null pointer reference in 1965. He did it because it was so easy to implement. He has called it his "billion-dollar mistake."

If you take the view that every variable has to have a value, and every method has to return something, then you need null (or None in Python). This is problematical for two reasons. First, if you send a message to an object, and that object happens to be null or None, an error will result. Second, if the variable or return value is numeric, null cannot be used; some numeric value must be chosen.

An alternative view is that some methods may return an *optional value*. In strongly typed languages, this means that the value is wrapped in a new type (Optional in Java and Option in Scala). The compiler then enforces type checking, so that an optional value cannot be used unless a value is actually present. Effectively, this converts run-time errors into syntax errors, which are much easier to deal with.

DOI: 10.1201/9781003358541-10

10.1 OPTIONAL IN PYTHON

Python does not have a way of representing optional values. Instead, the special value None indicates that a variable or expression has no value.

None is the single value of the type NoneType. Because Python is dynamic, the types of variables are not fixed; they have the type of whatever value they contain. Hence, a function that is expected to return a numeric value can return None instead.

Of course, the use of None in an expression where a number or object is required will still result in an error.

10.2 OPTIONAL IN JAVA

Every Java programmer is familiar with the NullPointerException. This problem can be avoided by using the Optional class.

Optional is a wrapper for objects. An Optional object may contain another object, or it may be empty. While this adds some complexity in the short run, working with optional objects turns out to be both easier and safer than working with objects that may or may not be null.

Optional has no constructors. Instead, there are three static methods in the Optional class of java.util:

- Optional.of(*v*) wraps the non-null value *v*. It causes a NullPointerException if *v* is null.

- Optional.ofNullable(*v*) returns either an Optional that contains a non-null value *v* or it returns an empty Optional.

- Optional.empty() returns an empty Optional.

Optional can, and generally should, have a type parameter. If s is a String, the following two statements are equivalent:

```
Optional<String> a = Optional.of(s);
Optional        a = Optional.of(s);
```

Some of the additional methods on Optional objects include:

- boolean equals(Object *obj*). Of course, all objects have an equals method, but this works correctly even if the Optional object contains null.

- boolean isPresent() returns true if the Optional isn't empty.

- void ifPresent(Consumer *c*) sends the value, if there is one, to the Consumer; otherwise, it does nothing.

- *T* get() returns the value or throws a No Such Element Exception if there isn't one.

- *T* orElse(*T other*) returns the value or returns *other* if there isn't a value.

- *T* orElseGet(Supplier *other*) returns the value, or if there is none, gets a value from the Supplier *other*.

Doubles, Integers, and Longs cannot be null. To wrap these numeric types, there are three more classes in java.util, namely,

- OptionalDouble

- OptionalInt

- OptionalLong.

Each of the numeric option classes has all the same methods, with two differences. There is no ofNullable method in these classes, and the get() method is replaced by getAsDouble(), getAsInt(), or getAsLong().

10.3 OPTION IN SCALA

Option is used when an operation may or may not succeed in returning a value.

Option is a parameterized type, so one may have, for example, an Option[String] type. The possible values of this type are Some(*value*), where the *value* is of the correct type, or None, for the case where no value has been found.

Example: val gender = Some("male")

Although a few operations are defined for Option types, it is far more common to use a match expression to extract the value, if one exists.

```
gender match {
  case Some(g) => println("Gender is " + g)
  case None => println("Gender unknown")
}
```

The above code tests whether gender is a Some or a None, and if it is a Some, the value g is extracted and used.

NullPointerExceptions happen in Java when a variable is used before being defined. Scala requires all variables to be given a value when they are declared, thus eliminating one source of NullPointerExceptions.

In Java, any method that returns an object could conceivably return null instead. The only way to be sure that it doesn't is to examine the method code carefully. In Scala, if a method might or might not return a result, it returns an Option. An Option is a type, and Scala does thorough type checking. If an Option[String] is used where a String is required, the error is caught at compile time.

Scala has a null value so that it can interface with Java. There is no other reason to ever use that value.

## CHAPTER 11

Lists

I N A PURELY FUNCTIONAL language, all data is considered to be immutable. Hence, every modification to a data structure results in yet another immutable data structure. This could quickly use up all available memory. This problem is mitigated in two ways:

- Data structures that are no longer reachable are automatically garbage collected.

- Data structures are **persistent**: a modification to an existing data structure results in the unmodified parts being shared by both the new and the old versions of that data structure.

The **singly linked list** (often referred to as just a **list**) is the most important data structure in a functional programming. It is simple to implement, and the four basic operations on a

DOI: 10.1201/9781003358541-11

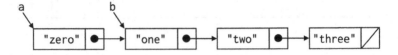

FIGURE 11.1   Lists are persistent data structures.

list automatically result in immutability and structure sharing. Those operations are:

- head returns the first value in the list.

- tail returns the part of the list starting right after the head.

- cons adds a value to the beginning of the list.

- isEmpty tests whether the list is empty.

In Figure 11.1, list a can be formed by "cons-ing" the value "zero" onto list b, and list b can be formed by taking the tail of list a. These operations, and any operations built from these, do not modify the existing lists.

Persistent data structures are key to concurrent programming. If all values are immutable, then there is no need for a locking mechanism to guarantee exclusive access to shared data, and an entire class of synchronization problems simply vanishes.

Functional programs use persistent data structures, especially singly linked lists, far more than arrays. Other persistent data structures are much more difficult to implement; a good functional programming language will provide some of these, rather than leaving implementation up to the programmer.

11.1 RECURSION

Recursion is to lists what iteration is to arrays. Any computation that can be done by iterating through an array can also be done by recursing through a list, and vice versa.

If you are not familiar with recursion, it requires a somewhat different way of thinking about a problem. Almost all recursive functions on lists follow a simple pattern: *Do something with the head, and recur with the tail. Stop the recursion when the tail is empty.*

The following are some examples of recursion, going from easiest to most complicated. To make the examples as readable as possible, the examples are in Scala but with the type information deleted. Recall that in Scala, no return statement is needed; the last value computed is the value returned.

To find the last element of a nonempty list:

```
def last(list) =
  if (list.tail.isEmpty) list.head
  else last(list.tail)
```

To add up all the numbers in a list:

```
def sum(list) =
  if (list.isEmpty) 0
  else list.head + sum(list.tail)
```

To double all the elements in a list:

```
def double(list) =
  if (list.isEmpty) List()
  else cons(2 * list.head, double(list.tail))
```

To append two lists:

```
def append(list1, list2) = {
  if (list1.isEmpty) list2
  else cons(list1.head, append(list1.tail, list2))
}
```

To reverse a list:

```
def reverse(list) =
  rev_helper(list, List())

def rev_helper(list, acc) =
  if (list.isEmpty) acc
  else rev_helper(list.tail, cons(list.head, acc))
```

The append and reverse functions, although short, are actually quite complex. Most recursive functions you are likely to write will be longer but simpler.

11.2 LISTS IN PYTHON

Python has a data structure called a "list," but this is a misnomer. Python lists are not implemented as lists, either as singly linked lists or as doubly linked lists; they are a more complex data structure based on arrays. The resultant data structure has many advantages, but it is not immutable.

As a consequence, Python does not have the usual head and tail operations, which access parts of the list but do not modify it. To simulate these, the programmer can write functions that take both (1) the list and (2) an index into the list, indicating which location is currently considered to be the head. It might be convenient to combine these into a tuple.

Operations that involve stepping through a Python list should be done using indices, which are far more efficient than repeatedly copying parts of the list.

There are packages available to provide persistent, singly linked lists for Python, and the interested reader is encouraged to seek these out. Alternatively, it is not difficult to create a simple List class in Python.

11.3 LISTS IN JAVA

Java has a List interface that does not have head and tail operations. Lists in Java are doubly linked, not singly linked, and are
backed by an array, so they are not *persistent*: they cannot share
structure. This is a good design for iterating (looping) through a
list but is less convenient for recursion.

To recurse through a list (or an array) in Java, the programmer
can write methods that take both (1) the list or array and (2) an
index, indicating which location is currently considered to be the
head.

As with Python, it is not difficult to create a singly linked list class
in Java. Such a class should implement the four basic operations
(head, tail, cons, isEmpty) and could include any methods
that can be built from these four.

11.4 LISTS IN SCALA

Scala has persistent singly linked lists.

A literal list is written in Scala as List(*value1*, *value2*, ..., *valueN*). The empty list is written as List() or as Nil.

All values in the list should be of the same type; if mixed types,
the type of the list is a type that can contain all the given values.
For example, List(5, 3.14) has type List[Double].

There are a few operations that can be considered basic to any use
of lists. These operations are very efficient (they take constant
time).

- *list*.head is the first value in *list*. It is an error if *list* is empty.

- *list*.tail is the rest of *list* after the head. It is an error if *list*
  is empty.

- *value* :: *list* returns a list whose head is *value* and whose tail is *list*. (The :: operator is pronounced "cons.")

- *list*.isEmpty returns true if *list* has no values.

The following operations are less efficient because they involve stepping through the list from beginning to end.

- *list*.length returns the number of elements in *list*.

- *list*.last returns the last element of *list*.

To preserve immutability, the following operations (except drop) require copying all or part of a list.

- *list*.init returns a list with the last element removed.

- *list*.take(*n*) returns a list of the first *n* elements. Especially useful for *lazy lists* (lists that generate elements only as needed).

- *list*.drop(*n*) returns a list with the first *n* elements removed.

- *list1* ::: *list2* appends the two lists.

- *list*.reverse returns a list in the reverse order.

- *list*.splitAt(*n*) returns the tuple (*list* take *n*, *list* drop *n*).

  - A *tuple* is an ordered list of values enclosed in parentheses.

  - Dots and parentheses may often be omitted when there is no ambiguity.

- *list1*.zip(*list2*) returns a list of tuples, where the first tuple contains the first element of *list1* and the first element of *list2*, the second tuple contains the second element of *list1* and the second element of *list2*, and so forth. The length of the result is the length of the shorter list.

- *list*.mkString(*str*) converts each element of *list* into a string and concatenates them with the string *str* in between elements.

- *list*.distinct returns a list with duplicated elements removed.

- *listOfLists*.flatten takes a list of lists of elements and returns a list of elements.

- *list* :+ *value* returns a new list with *value* appended to the end.

- *value* +: *list* returns a new list with *value* prepended to the beginning.

Scala's lists are immutable; none of the above operations alter the given list. When a list is returned as the result of an operation on a list, it may share structure with the given list.

## CHAPTER 12

Streams

A *STREAM* IS A MEANS of providing a sequence of values, one at a time, as needed. These values may come from an array, a collection, a file, or they may be generated. A stream is not itself a data structure, but it may get the values it returns from a data structure.

Because the values are only provided as needed, streams may be infinite. For example, you might have a stream of all the natural numbers, 1, 2, 3, … .

The main advantage of streams over lists is that not all values need be present in memory at the same time. The disadvantage is that it is easy to write a program that uses all the values in an infinite stream, resulting in an infinite loop.

Streams are useful in building *pipelines*. A pipeline is a sequence of operations applied to each element of a stream, only taking elements from the stream as needed.

Streams should not be confused with I/O streams.

DOI: 10.1201/9781003358541-12

12.1 GENERATORS IN PYTHON

Python doesn't have streams, but it has other ways of producing a sequence of values as needed. An iterator can be used to produce a sequence of values from a data structure, while a generator can compute a sequence of values as needed.

A *generator* is a function that contains a yield statement. This is like a return statement, except that the position and state of the function is "remembered"—the next call to the generator will resume execution right after the yield statement.

Here is a function that returns a generator. The first use of the generator will return the initial value, *init*. Each subsequent call will return the next larger integer.

```
def fromN(init):
    n = init
    while True:
        yield n
        n = n + 1

gen = fromN(1)
for i in range(0, 5):
    print(next(gen))
```

The call to fromN returns a generator, not an integer. The generator is saved in a variable named gen. After that, calls to next(gen) will return 1 (the value given for *init*), then 2, then 3, and so on.

> **Note:** The keyword yield also occurs in Scala but with a different meaning. Don't confuse the two.

12.2 STREAMS IN JAVA

A Stream is an interface (defined in java.util.stream). As with all interfaces, there are no constructors for streams. Instead, there are various methods that will return a stream. Here are some of them:

- `Stream.of(`*array*`)`, where *array* is an array of objects. (See s1 below.)

- `Arrays.stream(`*array*`)`, where *array* is an array of objects. (See s2 below.)

- `Stream.of(`*value1*, *value2*, ..., *valueN*`)` returns a `Stream` of those values. (See s3 below.)

- `Stream.of(`*list*`)`, where *list* is a `List`. (See s4 below.)

- *coll*`.stream()`, where *coll* is any type of `Collection`, such as `ArrayList`, `LinkedList`, or `HashSet` (see s5 below.)

- With a `StreamBuilder`: (see s6 below.)

  - Create an empty `StreamBuilder` with `Stream.builder()`,

  - Add values to it with `accept`, and

  - Get the resultant stream with `build()`.

Here are some examples of stream creation:

```
String[] langs = { "Python", "Java", "Scala" };
Stream s1 = Stream.of(langs);
Stream s2 = Arrays.stream(langs);
Stream s3 = Stream.of("Python", "Java", "Scala");
Stream s4 = Arrays.asList(langs).stream();
Stream s5 = new HashSet(Arrays.asList(langs)).
stream();

Stream.Builder builder = Stream.builder();
builder.accept("Python");
builder.accept("Java");
builder.accept("Scala");
Stream s6 = builder.build();
```

To anticipate a bit, we can print out the contents of streams s1 through s6 with code such as the following:

```
s5.forEach(s -> System.out.println(s));
```

The results will be the same in each case (except for using HashSet, in which the order of the results may be different).

Here are some other ways of creating a stream:

- Stream.empty() returns an empty stream.
- Stream.iterate(*seed*, *unaryOperator*) returns an infinite stream in which the unaryOperator is iteratively applied to the seed.
  - **Example**: Stream.iterate(1.0, (Double d) -> d / 2) gives the infinite stream 1.0, 0.5, 0.25, 0.125, etc.
- Stream.generate(*supplier*) returns an infinite stream in which the values are provided by the supplier.
  - **Example**: Stream.generate(Math::random) will return an infinite stream of random numbers.
- *collection*.parallelStream() returns a stream in which the elements could potentially be accessed in arbitrary order.

Streams are generally ordered, in the sense that there is a definite first element, a definite second element, and so on. Operations performed on an ordered stream, even if those operations are done in parallel, will produce an ordered result. The method *stream*.unordered() removes this constraint. The stream it returns is not changed in any way, except that parallel operations are now allowed to produce their results in any order.

12.3 NUMERIC STREAMS IN JAVA

The standard streams all contain objects. For efficiency, there are three numeric streams: IntStream, LongStream, and DoubleStream. As with general streams, there are no constructors for numeric streams; rather, there are methods that return numeric streams.

We illustrate with IntStream:

- IntStream.empty() returns an empty IntStream.

- IntStream.of(*int1*, *int2*, ..., *intN*) returns an IntStream containing the given integers.

- IntStream.range(*start*, *end*) returns an IntStream of the integers from *start* up to but not including *end*. Oddly, there is no version of range that has a third *step* parameter.

- *intStream*.boxed() returns a Stream<Integer> of the boxed int values in *intStream*.

Most of the methods on a Stream are also available on an IntStream: count, distinct, filter, etc. There are some differences; for example, max, min, and sorted do not require a Comparator as an argument.

Comparable methods are available for LongStream and DoubleStream.

12.4 STREAMS IN SCALA

There are several ways to create a stream in Scala. Most collections have a toStream method.

- List(1, 2, 3).toStream
- Set(1, 2, 3).toStream
- Array(1, 2, 3).toStream

- Range(1, 10).toStream
- (1 to 10).toStream
  - This is shorthand for Range(1, 10).toStream
- (1 to 10 by 2).toStream

The Stream object provides a number of ways to create a stream. Here are just a few:

```
Steam.empty
Stream.range(start, end, step)
```

- Stream.from(*start*)

  - Produces an infinite stream of integers starting with *start* and adding 1 each time.

- Stream.from(*start, step*)

  - Produces an infinite stream of integers starting with *start* and adding *step* each time.

- Stream.iterate(*start*)(*function*)

  - Produces an infinite stream of integers starting with *start* and applying *function* each time. (The two parameter lists indicate a *curried function*; see Section 8.3.)

  - **Example**: Stream.iterate(2)(n => 2 * n) produces the stream 2, 4, 8, 16, 32, and so on.

## CHAPTER 13

Important Functions

THERE ARE THREE HIGHER-ORDER functions that may, in some sense, be considered fundamental. A great many other higher-order functions can be constructed with them. They are:

- map — Applies a function to each element of a list, producing a list of results of the same length as the given list.

- filter — Applies a predicate to each element of a list, discarding each element that fails the predicate, resulting in a potentially shorter list.

- fold or reduce — Produces a single value based on the contents of a list. The distinction between these two functions is that reduce will provide a default value if given an empty list.

The following sections describe the Python, Java, and Scala versions of these methods. Scala has a particularly rich set of higher-order functions, which are described in Section 14.4; you

DOI: 10.1201/9781003358541-13

may wish to peruse these, even if you have no particular interest in Scala, because you may find it useful to implement them in your preferred language.

13.1 IMPORTANT FUNCTIONS IN PYTHON

Three important higher-order functions are map, filter, and reduce.

- map(*function*, *list*) returns an iterator for a new list of the same length as *list*. It does this by applying *function* to each element of *list*.

- filter(*test*, *list*) returns an iterator for a new list that is potentially shorter than *list*. It does this by applying *test* to each generated element of *list* and discarding those values for which *test* is false.

- reduce(*function*, *list*, *initial_value*) returns a single value. If *list* is empty, the result is *initial_value*; otherwise, the *function* (which must have two parameters) is applied pairwise to the values in the *list*, starting with *initial_value* and *list*[0]. Each application of *function* results in a value, which is then combined with the next value in *list*.

Examples, where lst is [1, 2, 3, 4, 5, 6]:

```
list(map(lambda x: 10 * x, lst))
# Result is [10, 20, 30, 40, 50, 60]

list(map(lambda x: (x, x * x), lst))
# Result is [(1, 1), (2, 4), (3, 9), (4, 16),
(5, 25), (6, 36)]

list(filter(lambda x: x % 2 == 0, lst))
# Result is [2, 4, 6]

reduce(lambda x, y: x * y, lst, 1)
# Result is 720
```

Python also has decorators. A *decorator* is a means of intercepting a call to a function, so that when the program attempts to call the function, control is instead given to a decorator of that function. For example,

```
def trace(fun):
    def wrapper(a, b):
      print("Calling", fun.__name__,
       "with", a, b)
      result = fun(a, b)
      print(" Returning", result)
      return result
    return wrapper

@trace
def multiply(x, y):
    return x * y
```

With this code, a call to multiply(5, 7) will return 35 as usual but will also print the following:

```
Calling multiply with 5 7
  Returning 35
```

The name trace isn't special; any name will do, so long as the annotation on the function multiply matches the name of the decorating function. Note that the function wrapper, defined inside trace, has the same number of parameters as multiply.

Decorators in Python are quite simple to construct, because variables do not have a fixed type; their type is the type of the value that happens to be in them at the time. While it is possible to construct decorators in Java and Scala, that is beyond the scope of this book.

13.2 IMPORTANT FUNCTIONS IN JAVA

Java has versions of the more important higher-order functions: map, flatMap, filter, and reduce. These work only with streams, so to use them with any collection, that collection must first be converted to a stream, and the results converted back to a collection.

While it is generally true that generic types in Java need not be parameterized (for example, you can use List for a list of integers rather than List<Integer>), this no longer appears to be true for streams. Type parameters have been omitted in most of this book, but not in this section.

Here are some initial declarations:

```
List<Integer> numbers = Arrays.asList(1,2,3,4,5);
Stream<Integer> nums = numbers.stream();
```

Each of the following examples uses the stream nums. Since printing the results uses up the stream, nums must be reassigned before each example.

Map applies a function to each element of a stream, producing a stream of results. In this first example, map is used to double each number in stream nums.

```
Stream<Integer> squares = nums.map(n -> n * 2);
List<Integer> res1 =
    squares.collect(Collectors.toList());
System.out.println(res1);
    // Prints map: [2, 4, 6, 8, 10]
```

The next two examples demonstrate the difference between map and flatMap. For a stream of streams, flatMap "flattens" the result by moving the elements in a sub-level up to the top level.

Since it is not easy in a single Java expression to create a stream of integer arrays, we first define a method to do this.

```
public static Stream<Integer> powers(Integer x) {
    List<Integer> list = new ArrayList<Integer>();
    list.add(x);
    list.add(x * x);
    return list.stream();
}
```

We can use this to create a stream of streams of integers, each sub-stream containing a given number along with its square.

```
Stream<Stream<Integer>> ssi = nums.map(n -> powers(n));
```

Then, collect and print the results:

```
Stream<ArrayList<Integer>> sal =
    ssi.map(x -> (ArrayList<Integer>)
        x.collect(Collectors.toList()));
List<List<Integer>> csal =
    sal.collect(Collectors.toList());
System.out.println("map: " + csal);
  // Prints map: [[1, 1], [2, 4], [3, 9], [4, 16],
  [5, 25]]
```

Using flatMap produces the same numbers but in a flattened list.

```
nums = numbers.stream();
Stream<Integer> si = nums.flatMap(n -> powers(n));
ArrayList<Integer> ali = (ArrayList<Integer>)
si.collect(Collectors.toList());
System.out.println("flatMap: " + ali);
  // Prints flatMap: [1, 1, 2, 4, 3, 9, 4, 16, 5, 25]
```

The filter method is used with a predicate to "filter out" from the stream elements that do not satisfy the predicate. In this example, we select only even numbers.

```
Stream<Integer> evens = nums.filter(n -> n % 2 == 0);
List<Integer> res2 = evens.collect(Collectors.
toList());
System.out.println("filter: " + res2);
  // Prints filter: [2, 4]
```

Finally, reduce is used to combine all the values in a stream into a single value. In this example, the numbers are combined by adding them.

```
int sum1 = nums.reduce(0, (x, y) -> x + y);
System.out.println("reduce: " + sum1);
  // Prints reduce: 15
```

13.3 IMPORTANT FUNCTIONS IN SCALA

A number of higher-order functions in Scala are of special importance.

For the examples below, assume that list has the value List(1, 2, 3, 4, 5). The result of each function call is shown after the call.

- ***list*.map(*function*)** returns a list in which the function of one argument has been applied to each element.

  - list.map(x => x * x)

    - List(1, 4, 9, 16, 25)

  - list.map(x => List(x, x * x))

    - List(List(1, 1), List(2, 4), List(3, 9), List(4, 16), List(5, 25))

- ***listOfLists*.flatMap(*function*)** returns a list in which the function of one argument has been applied to each element of each sublist. It removes one "level" of nesting.

  - list.flatMap(x => List(x, x * x))

    - List(1, 1, 2, 4, 3, 9, 4, 16, 5, 25)

  - Compare this with list.map(x => List(x, x * x)) above.

- *list*.filter(*predicate*) returns a list of the elements of the given list for which the predicate is true.

  - list.filter(x => x % 2 == 0)

    - List(2, 4)

The following functions reduce a list to a single value.

- *nonempty_list*.reduceLeft(*binary_function*) applies the function to each pair of elements of *list*, using each function result as the new first argument to the function and returns the final value. It is an error if *list* is empty.

- *nonempty_list*.reduceRight(*binary_function*) is the same as reduceLeft, except that it starts from the right end of the list, using each function result as the new second argument to the function.

- *list*.foldLeft(*value*)(*binary_function*) does what reduceLeft would do if *value* were appended to the beginning of *list*. If *list* is empty, *value* is returned.

- *list*.foldRight(*value*)(*binary_function*) does what reduce-Right would do if *value* were appended to the end of *list*. If *list* is empty, *value* is returned.

Examples:

- list.reduceLeft((a, b) => a + b) // (((1-2)-3)-4)-5 = 15
- list.reduceRight((a, b) => a + b) // 1-(2-(3-(4-5))) = 15
- list.foldLeft(0)((a, b) => a + b) // ((((0-1)-2)-3)-4)-5 = 15
- list.foldRight(0)((a, b) => a + b) // 1-(2-(3-(4-(5-0)))) = 15
- list.reduceLeft((a, b) => a - b) // (((1-2)-3)-4)-5 = -13
- list.reduceRight((a, b) => a - b) // 1-(2-(3-(4-5))) = 3

- `list.foldLeft(0)((a, b) => a - b)` // `((((0-1)-2)-3)-4)-5 = -15`

- `list.foldRight(0)((a, b) => a - b)` // `1-(2-(3-(4-(5-0)))) = 3`

In a previous section, we discussed for comprehensions. These are actually implemented as a combination of the functions `map`, `filter`, and `flatMap`.

These two expressions are equivalent:

```
for (w <- words if ! w.contains('v')) yield
w.toUpperCase

words.filter(w => ! w.contains('v')).map(w =>
w.toUpperCase)
```

If words has the value `List("Python", "Java", "Scala")`, each of the above would result in `List("PYTHON", "SCALA")`.

When there is more than one generator, `flatMap` is also used. The following expressions are equivalent:

```
for (w <- words; c <- w) yield c.toUpper

words.flatMap(w => w.toUpperCase)
```

and both result in `List("P", "Y", "T", "H", "O", "N", "J", "A", "V", "A", "S", "C", "A", "L", "A")`.

The functions `foldLeft`, `foldRight`, `reduceLeft`, and `reduceRight` are all means of reducing a list to a single value. For example, the following expression will return the longest word in a list of words.

```
words.foldLeft("")((a, b) => if (a.length > b.length) a
else b)
```

13.4 ADDITIONAL FUNCTIONS IN SCALA

Here are some additional higher-order functions in Scala. Where an example is given, it is in the same form as the examples in the previous section.

- *list*.collect *partial_function* returns a list of the results of the partial function, filtering out those where the partial function does not apply.

  - A *partial function* is a function that is not necessarily defined for every possible input.

- *list*.dropWhile(*predicate*) returns a list omitting those values at the front of the given list that satisfy the predicate.

- *list*.exists(*predicate*) returns true if any element of the list satisfies the predicate.

- *list*.filterNot(*predicate*) returns a list of the elements of the given list for which the predicate is false.

- *list*.find(*predicate*) returns, as Some(*value*), the first value in the list that satisfies the predicate, or None if no such value is found.

- *list*.forall(*predicate*) returns true if every element of the list satisfies the predicate.

- *list*.groupBy(*function*) returns a Map of keys to values, where the keys are the results of applying the function to each list element, and the values are a List of values in the list such that applying the function to that value yields that key.

  - List("one", "two", "three").groupBy(x => x.length)

  - Result is Map(5 -> List(three), 3 -> List(one, two))

- *list*.indexWhere(*predicate*) returns the index of the first value in the list that satisfies the predicate, or -1 if no such value is found.

- *list*.indexWhere(***predicate, start***) returns the index of the first value in the list at or after ***start*** that satisfies the predicate, or -1 if no such value is found.

- *list*.lastIndexWhere(***predicate***) returns the index of the last value in the list that satisfies the predicate, or -1 if no such value is found.

- *list*.lastIndexWhere(***predicate, end***) returns the index of the last value before ***end*** in the list that satisfies the predicate, or -1 if no such value is found.

- *list*.partition(***predicate***) returns a tuple of two lists: a list of values that satisfy the predicate, and a list of those that do not.

- *list*.scan(***e***)(***binary_function***) returns a list of cumulative values starting with ***e***, where each successive value is computed by applying the function to the current value and the next element.

  - *list*.scan(0)((a, b) => a + b) computes a running total. Applied to List(1, 2, 3, 4, 5), the result will be List(0, 1, 3, 6, 10, 15).

- *list*.sortWith(***comparisonFunction***) sorts a list using the two-parameter comparison function.

  - *list*.sortWith((a, b) => a > b) sorts *list* in descending order.

- *list*.span(***predicate***) returns a tuple of two lists: a list of all the values at the front of the list that satisfy the predicate, and a list containing all the remaining values. In other words, span is a combination of takeWhile and dropWhile.

- *list*.takeWhile(***predicate***) returns a list of the values at the front of the given list that satisfy the predicate, stopping short of the first value that does not.

## CHAPTER 14

Pipelines

A N IMPORTANT USE OF streams is the creation of *pipelines*. Pipelines provide a (relatively) easy way to do some parallel processing. To give some insight into the nature of a pipeline, we start with a nonprogramming example.

Around Easter, some people like to create a basket of colorful eggs. To do this, one first has to purchase eggs. The eggs are then hard-cooked. Next, they are put into cups containing various colors of egg dye. The eggs are then taken out and allowed to dry before being put into a basket. As a pipeline, the process looks something like this:

```
purchase egg → cook egg → dye egg → dry egg → put
egg in basket
```

This could be done one egg at a time, but it wouldn't be very efficient. The eggs could be bought all at once, and they could be cooked in several batches, depending on the size of pot available. There could be several cups, each containing a different color of dye, so eggs could be dyed different colors simultaneously, or an egg might have to wait until the desired color becomes available. Eggs can be taken out to dry as soon as they have reached the desired color, and they can be put in the basket once they are dry. Clearly, a lot of parallelism is possible.

Here's how a pipeline works:

1. **A stream of values is created**. The values might already exist, for example, in an array or a list, and the stream simply provides them. Or the values may be generated as required, perhaps by a mathematical function. In the egg example, we might consider purchasing the eggs as providing the initial stream.

2. Zero or more **intermediate operations** are applied to the stream. Each intermediate operation takes a value from the stream it is given, applies some operation to it, and gives the result to the next stream in the sequence. Not all values need be passed along; some may be discarded. In the egg example, cooking, dying, and drying are the intermediate operations, and we might discard any eggs that crack when they are cooked.

3. A **terminal operation** takes a stream and produces a final result (a basket of eggs).

Assuming that all the eggs have been purchased, one way to do this is to cook the first egg, dye it, dry it, put it in the basket, and then proceed with the second egg. This is not necessarily how the pipeline works.

Another way is to cook the second egg while the first egg is being dyed; then to cook the third egg while the first egg is drying and the second egg is being dyed; and so on. Again, this is not necessarily how the pipeline works.

If, for example, eggs are slow to dye but quick to dry, then possibly there are periods when no eggs are being dried. Meanwhile, there may be cooked eggs waiting for an opportunity to be dyed. This is the most likely way the pipeline works. Operations may be performed in parallel but only when their inputs are available.

Pipelines operate on a "pull," rather than a "push" basis. Intermediate operations are said to be *lazy*—they perform only when a subsequent operation demands input. According to the Java API (application programming interface) documentation, "execution begins when the terminal operation is invoked, and ends when the terminal operation completes." (The process might stop when the egg basket is full, leaving uncooked and undyed eggs.)

Intermediate operations may be stateless or stateful. A ***stateful*** operation is one whose operation depends on something that might change during the course of the pipeline (for example, the egg dye gets used up); this may cause nondeterministic or incorrect results. A ***stateless*** operation is a pure function; its output depends only on its input, so given the same input again, it will produce the same result.

14.1 PIPELINES IN PYTHON

In order to use pipelines in Python, a third-party package such as scinkit-learn or the Apache Beam SDK must be installed. These are somewhat complex and are not covered in this book. Here, we just note that a suitable pipeline could look something like this:

```
basket = for_each(egg)
        .purchase()
        .cook()
        .dye()
        .dry()
        .collect()
```

This is approximately the same as saying

```
basket = []
for egg in eggs:
    basket.append(dry(dye(cook(purchase(egg)))))
```

There is a minor difference in readability and a more significant difference in how easily the operations can be done in parallel.

14.2 PIPELINES IN JAVA

A *stream* consists of three parts: A **supplier**, to provide initial values; zero or more **intermediate operations**, to perform transformations on those values; and a **terminal operation**, to produce a final result.

Earlier sections described various ways a stream may be created (with Stream.of(*list*), for example). The following sections will cover intermediate and terminal operations.

14.2.1 Intermediate Operations

An ***intermediate operation*** is one that takes a Stream as input and produces a Stream as output. All intermediate streams are *lazy*; they don't produce a value until the next operation in the pipeline requests one.

- filter(*predicate*) returns a stream containing all the values that satisfy the predicate, and none of the values that fail the predicate.

- map(*function*) returns a stream in which each element is the result of applying the function to the corresponding input element.

- distinct() returns a stream in which no element occurs more than once (according to the equals method).

- sorted() returns a stream in which the elements of the input stream are returned according to their natural ordering.

- sorted(*comparator*) returns a stream in which the elements of the input stream are returned in the order defined by the *comparator*.

- peek(*consumer*) returns the elements of the given stream, with the added feature that the element is sent to the consumer. This is useful when debugging.

- limit(*maxSize*) returns the elements of the given stream, stopping after *maxSize* elements.

- skip(*maxSize*) returns this stream after discarding the first *maxSize* elements.

One additional intermediate operation, flatMap, requires additional explanation.

The flatMap(*function*) requires that *function*, when applied to each element of the given stream, produces another stream. If such a function were given to map, it would produce a stream of streams. The flatMap function, however, "flattens" its output into a single stream.

A pair of examples should help clarify this.

```
Stream.of(1, 2, 3)
  .map(x -> Stream.of(x, x*x, x*x*x))
  .forEach(y -> System.out.println(
    Arrays.toString(y.toArray()) ));
```

When executed, the above code produces three lines: [1, 1, 1], [2, 4, 8], and [3, 9, 27]. Replacing map with flatMap produces a result which is simpler to print:

```
Stream.of(1, 2, 3)
  .flatMap(x -> Stream.of(x, x*x, x*x*x))
  .forEach(y -> System.out.println(y));
```

In this case, the result (on nine lines) is 1 1 1 2 4 8 3 9 27.

14.2.2 Terminal Operations

A *terminal operation* is one that takes a Stream as input but does not produce a Stream as output; thus, it terminates a pipeline. The terminal operation may return a value of some other type, or it may return void.

Possibly the simplest terminal operation is forEach, which was used in an earlier section. An example is:

```
Stream s3 = Stream.of("Python", "Java", "Scala");
s3.forEach(s -> System.out.println(s));
```

The argument of forEach must be a Consumer type, that is, a function that takes an argument but whose return type is void.

Besides streams, forEach can be invoked on any Iterable objects, such as lists and maps.

A stream can only be used once; after that, it is used up. If, for example, you tried to do anything more with stream s3 above, you would get the message IllegalStateException: stream has already been operated upon or closed.

Some operations, such as max, are nonterminating if applied to an infinite stream.

Most operations are nondeterministic when used with a parallel stream. For example, multiple threads may share in the processing of a forEach operation, so that every element gets processed, but not necessarily in order.

Here is an alphabetical list of terminal operations defined by the Stream interface:

- allMatch(*predicate*) returns a boolean indicating whether every element of this stream satisfies the predicate (returns true if the stream is empty). If an element is found that does not satisfy the predicate, no further elements are processed.

- anyMatch(*predicate*) returns true if any element of this stream satisfies the predicate. If such an element is found, no further elements are processed.

- collect(*collector*) and collect(*collector, biconsumer1, biconsumer2*) return a collection of results. Collectors will be discussed in the next section.

- count() returns the number of elements in this stream.

- findAny() returns an Optional containing an arbitrary element of this stream or an empty Optional if the stream is empty. No further elements are processed.

- findFirst() returns an Optional containing the first element of this stream or an empty Optional if this stream is empty. No further elements are processed. The operation is deterministic if the stream is ordered.

- forEach(*consumer*) performs the consumer's SAM (Single Abstract Method) for every element of this stream, not necessarily in order.

- forEachOrdered(*consumer*) performs the consumer's SAM for every element of the sequence. If this stream is ordered, the actions are performed in order.

- max(*comparator*) returns the maximum element of this stream, according to the *comparator*.

- min(*comparator*) returns the minimum element of this stream, according to the *comparator*.

- noneMatch(**predicate**) returns true if there is no element of this stream that satisfies the predicate (returns true if the stream is empty). If an element is found that satisfies the predicate, no further elements are processed.

- reduce(**binaryOperator**) reduces the elements of this stream to a single value by repeated application of the binary operator. Because the operations may be applied in any order, the binary operator should be associative.

- toArray() returns an array containing the elements of this stream.

14.2.3 Collectors

Collectors are terminal operators that return a Collection of some sort, rather than a single value.

> **Note:** toArray() is not a collector because Java arrays do not implement the Collection interface.

> **Note:** Take care to distinguish between the Collector interface, the Collection interface, and the Collections class.

The simplest collector method is java.util.stream.collect (**collector**), in the Stream interface.

Here is a selection of suitable collectors from java.util.stream. Collectors:

- Collectors.toSet() returns a set.

- Collectors.toList() returns a list.

- toCollection(**constructorFunction**) returns a collection of the designated type, where the **constructorFunction** is a constructor wrapped as a function; for example, LinkedList::new.

- Collectors.partitioningBy(*predicate*) returns a Map in which the keys are true and false, and the values are ArrayLists of the values that do or do not satisfy the predicate.

- Collectors.groupingBy(*function*) returns a Map in which the keys are the results of the function, and the values are ArrayLists of the inputs to the function that produce the given key.

14.2.4 Example

Suppose you want to print all 5-digit numbers that (a) are palindromes and (b) whose digits sum to 20. It can be done as follows:

```
Stream.iterate(10000, n -> n + 1)
    .limit(90000)
    .map(n -> n.toString())
    .filter(s -> s.equals(reverse(s)))
    .filter(s ->
      s.chars()
        .map(Character::getNumericValue)
          .sum() == 20)
      .forEach(s -> System.out.print(s + " "));
```

1. The iterate method creates an infinite stream of numbers, starting with 10000 and going up by one each time.

2. The limit method cuts off the stream after 90000 numbers (*not* after the number 90000). Most of the numbers will be discarded by a later filter operation.

3. The map method uses ToString to convert each number into a string.

4. The first filter method passes only those numbers whose string representation is unchanged when it is reversed. (The reverse method is given below.)

5. The second filter method passes only those strings whose digits sum to 20.

- s.chars() creates a stream of Unicode values from string s.

- The map method uses getNumericValue to convert each Unicode value to the corresponding numeric value ('0' to 0, '1' to 1, etc.)

- The sum method adds all the digits, which are then compared to 20.

6. The forEach method prints all the values that remain. If we were to replace this with count() and print the result, we would find that there are 39 5-digit palindromes whose digits sum to 20.

The reverse method was programmed separately; it is:

```
static String reverse(String s) {
    return new StringBuilder(s)
              .reverse()
              .toString();
```

This method could have been incorporated into the pipeline, but it has been separated out for reasons of clarity.

The use of streams can make a program more readable. As with most features, misuse can make a program less readable. The second filter method in the above example demonstrates that a stream can be created and used within another stream, but this isn't necessarily a good idea. The code would be more readable if it used a separate digitSum method.

14.3 PIPELINES IN SCALA

Suppose you want to print all 5-digit numbers that (a) are palindromes and (b) whose digits sum to 20. (This is the same example we just did in Java.) Here is some code to do that.

```
println(Stream.range(10000, 1000000)
    .map(e => e.toString)
    .filter(e => e == e.reverse)
    .filter(e =>
        (e.toList).map(e => e.asDigit).sum == 20)
    .foreach(e => print(e + " "))
    )
```

Explanation:

1. The Stream.range(10000, 1000000) call will generate consecutive integers starting with 10000 and going up to 99999.

2. map(e => e.toString) will turn each number into a string.

3. filter(e => e == e.reverse) will reverse each string and discard it if it differs from the original string.

4. The next lines discard any numbers whose digits do not sum to 20.

   - (e.toList) turns the string into a list of characters.

   - map(e => e.asDigit) turns each character in the list into a single-digit number, returning a list of numbers.

   - sum adds the single-digit numbers in the list to produce a "digit sum" for the given 5-digit number

   - Any number whose digit sum is not 20 is discarded (filtered out).

5. foreach(e => print(e + " ")) applies the print function to each number in the resultant list (15851, 16661, 17471, ..., up to 109901).

## CHAPTER 15

Summary and Final Examples

ALTHOUGH SELDOM LISTED AS an advantage of functional programming, treating functions as values allows many if not most loops to be replaced by function calls. The purpose of a function call can often be understood at a glance, but this is seldom true of loops. The programmer usually has to examine each part of a loop to determine if it is correct.

A related issue is code duplication. Many loops in a typical program are very similar to one another. Most loops perform mapping, filtering, reduction, or some combination of these. If a loop can be specialized by simply supplying a function as a parameter, this commonality can be exploited.

The most important use of functional programming, however, is programming concurrency. Now that single-core machines are largely a thing of the past, the ability to write concurrent, multi-threaded programs is essential.

DOI: 10.1201/9781003358541-15

The traditional approach to concurrent programming is to share data among threads. When this is done, great care must be taken to prevent more than one thread from accessing any particular piece of data while another thread could possibly be modifying that same data. Failure to do this results in nondeterminism. The most common (and most serious) consequence is that errors are seldom discovered until the application has been deployed and gets significant use. This is a balancing act because the expense of protecting every bit of data in this way tends to obviate the value of concurrency.

Functional programming provides a different approach. Because data is immutable, it can be shared across threads with no problem. Because the data structures used are persistent (minor variants in the data structure share the common parts), memory requirements are feasible. In short, functional programming is a far safer and easier approach to concurrent programming.

This book is about functional programming, not concurrent programming. The goal has been to demonstrate the value of the functional approach in ordinary programming and to lay the groundwork for use in concurrency.

15.1 EXAMPLES IN PYTHON

Proper use of functional features makes programs easier to read and debug. Consider the following examples of code to find the minimum value in a list my_list:

```
least = my_list[0]

for i in range(1, len(my_list)):
    if least < my_list[i]:
        least = my_list[i]
```

compared to

```
least = reduce(lambda a, b: a if a < b else b, my_list)
```

The careful reader will have noticed that one of the above code blocks contains an error.

For a more extended example, the following code computes the checksum for an ISBN (International Standard Book Number). Rather than trying to describe the algorithm, we will let the code speak for itself.

Here is the traditional approach:

```python
def get_digits(number):
    """Given an int or string, return a list
        of the digits in it."""
    string = str(number)
    return [x for x in string if x.isdigit()]

def compute_isbn_13_checksum(number):
    """Given the first 12 digits (as an
        int or string) of an ISBN-13 number,
        compute the 13th (checksum) digit."""
    digits = get_digits(number)
    sum = 0
    for i in range(0, 12):
        if i % 2 == 0:
            sum += int(digits[i])
        else:
            sum += 3 * int(digits[i])
    mod = sum % 10
    return 0 if mod == 0 else 10 - mod
```

Here is a more functional approach:

```python
def isbn13_checksum(isbn):
    """Given the first 12 digits (as an
        int or string) of an ISBN-13 number,
        compute the 13th (checksum) digit."""
    digits = [int(x) for x in str(isbn) if
    x.isdigit()]
    addend = lambda i:
```

```
                    digits[i] if i % 2 == 0
                        else 3 * digits[i]
        mod = sum([addend(i)
                for i in range(0, 12)]) % 10
        return 0 if mod == 0 else 10 - mod
```

Both of the above methods have been tested and work correctly.

15.2 EXAMPLES IN JAVA

To find the minimum value in an array of integers, one could write:

```
static int least(int[] ary) {
  int least = ary[0];
  for (int i = 0; i < ary.length; i++) {
    if (ary[i] < least) least = ary[i];
  }
  return least;
}
System.out.println("Least is " + least(ary));
```

It might (or might not) be somewhat simpler to write:

```
System.out.println("Least is " +
  Arrays
    .stream(ary)
    .reduce(ary[0],
            (int x, int y) ->
              x < y ? x : y));
}
```

As in the Python example in the previous section, the alert reader will notice that the code with a loop contains an error.

As a longer example, the following code computes the checksum for an ISBN-13 (International Standard Book Number). This is a 12-digit number with the 13th number serving as a checksum.

```
/**
 * Given a 12 digit ISBN number, compute
   the 13th (checksum) digit.
 */
private static int isbn13_checksum(String s) {
  // Remove possible dashes
  String[] ss = s.replaceAll("-", "").split("");
  String[] odds = new String[6];
  String[] evens = new String[6];
  for (int i = 0; i < 6; i++) {
    odds[i] = ss[2 * i];
    evens[i] = ss[2 * i + 1];
  }
  Stream<Integer> oddstream =
    Stream.of(odds).map(x -> new Integer(x));
  Stream<Integer> evenstream =
    Stream.of(evens).map(x -> 3 * new Integer(x));

  int sum = Stream.concat(oddstream, evenstream)
         .reduce(0, (a, b) -> a + b);
  int mod = sum % 10;
  return mod == 0 ? 0 : 10 - mod;
}
```

There appears to be no way in Java to separate a stream into two distinct streams, so the first part of this method turns the input string into two separate arrays of strings.

It is difficult to argue that the use of streams and other functional features adds any clarity to the algorithm.

15.3 EXAMPLES IN SCALA

In Scala, it is natural to work with lists rather than arrays and with recursion rather than loops.

The minimum value in a list ls can be found recursively:

```
def least(ls: List[Int]): Int =
  if (ls.tail isEmpty) ls.head
  else {
    val lt = least(ls.tail)
    if (ls.head < lt) ls.head else lt
  }

println(least(ls))
```

Or the minimum value can be found with a reduce operation:

```
println(ls.reduceLeft((a, b) => if (a < b) a else b))
```

Or one can simply use the min function: `println(ls.min)`.

As a longer example, one can compute the checksum for an ISBN (International Standard Book Number) in a completely functional way with a pipeline:

```
def isbn13_checksum(isbn: String) = {
  val total = isbn
            .filter(c => c isDigit)
            .map(c => c.asDigit)
            .grouped(2).toList
            .map(p => p(0) + 3 * p(1))
            .sum
  val mod = total % 10
  if (mod == 0) 0 else 10 - mod
}
```

The grouped(2) function above returns a new list containing the first two elements of the given list, then the second two elements, and so on.

Afterword

I N WRITING THIS BOOK, I have tried to be as objective as possible. This section, however, reflects my personal, subjective views. The reader may have different views, in which case I hope we can disagree amicably.

Python is an excellent language, and the first one I go to for much of my programming. Its developer, Guido van Rossum, has been against adding functional programming to Python. The few FP features that he has added have been done extremely well and are very useful.

I have used Java extensively since its inception. It is a workhorse of a language. While it is overly verbose and has too many special cases, it was a breakthrough language in its time.

Throughout its history, the people continuing to develop Java have done a great job of adding new features in such a way as to break few or no existing programs. Adding some FP features to Java under these constraints was clearly a major effort and an impressive technical achievement. The addition of functions and the ability to use them with legacy code are definitely improvements.

I will freely admit that getting some of the Java examples in this book to work was a nightmare. It is very likely that someone more familiar with the FP features could write the same examples in a

DOI: 10.1201/9781003358541-16

simpler fashion. Personally, I remain unconvinced that many of the new features add anything useful to the language.

Scala was designed to be similar to Java, in order to make it easier for Java programmers to adopt the new language. (The similarity is not particularly evident in this book, because I have ignored the object-oriented features in favor of the functional features.) Some have argued that Scala is more difficult to learn than Java, but I have not found it so—certainly not if Java's functional features are included in the comparison!

The usual recommendation for programmers who wish to learn functional programming is to learn Haskell. Haskell is purely functional, and anyone who learns Haskell definitely understands functional programming.

My recommendation is somewhat different. Scala is a much easier language to learn and is much more practical in the real world. It has most of the features of Haskell but doesn't take away all the tools you already know; it just adds to them. It runs on the JVM (Java virtual machine). And it certainly isn't as verbose as Java.

I hope this slim volume has gotten you started on the road to being a functional programmer. Besides being a powerful technique, programming in a functional way is simply more fun.

Index

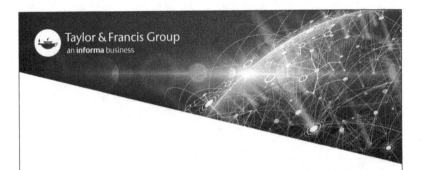

Printed in the United States
by Baker & Taylor Publisher Services